Tell a Tale of Iowa

Sleep, Old Pioneer!

Careless crowds go daily past you,
Where *their* future fate has cast you,
    Leaving not a sigh or tear;
And your wonder-works outlast you—
    Brave old pioneer!

But *our* memory-eyes have found you,
And we hold you grandly dear:
With no work-day woes to wound you—
With the peace of God around you—
    Sleep, old pioneer!

—Will Carleton
Farm Festivals, 1881

Tell a Tale of Iowa

By

Don Doyle Brown

Illustrations By
Ralph Moore

Published By
WALLACE-HOMESTEAD BOOK CO.
Des Moines, Iowa

Copyright, 1965
By
DON DOYLE BROWN
Leon, Iowa

First Printing, 1965
Second Printing, Paperback Edition, 1968
Third Printing, Paperback Edition, 1969
Fourth Printing, Paperback Edition, 1973

Cover Photo by Joan Liffring
Courtesy, *THE IOWAN* Magazine

PRINTED IN THE UNITED STATES OF AMERICA

Dedication

IN THE EARLY DAWN of November 20, 1968, near the tiny village of Tan My in Quang Tin Province, South Vietnam, Lt. Kevin G. Burke of Anita, Iowa, volunteered to lead a rescue mission to attempt to reach several men from another company who were pinned down by enemy fire.

Lieutenant Burke carried two injured men to safety and then charged the enemy fortification, again braving heavy fire, to attempt to rescue a seriously injured man who lay next to an enemy bunker. As he neared the wounded soldier a single enemy shot found its mark and instantly killed Lt. Kevin Burke.

At the age of 24, Kevin Burke, a son of Iowa, a star in athletics, an award winning public speaker, a graduate of Notre Dame, a man of many friends and a youth whose future held unbounded promise, died the death of a hero in a foreign land while trying to save the life of a man he didn't even know.

During his funeral on December 7, 1968, the anniversary of the start of another war, the whole town of Anita turned out in a solemn honor guard at a round the clock vigil to honor the memory of its fallen son. Later, the Department of the Army awarded Lieutenant Burke the Distinguished Service Cross, the nation's second highest military decoration, as well as the Bronze Star, Purple Heart and the Combat Infantryman's Badge.

This book then, is dedicated to the memory of Lt. Kevin G. Burke, who, by the manner in which he lived and by the manner in which he died, proved he was a hero all the way.

LT. KEVIN GAIL BURKE
1944 - 1968

Acknowledgments

The stories included in this book are all taken from a series of syndicated articles published in Iowa newspapers over a two-year period. Those chosen for this book were selected on the basis of popular reader response and what we felt were of general importance to the history of the state. These articles make no pretense at being scholarly or conclusive—but we hope they are all entertaining and informative. Some, such as the stories of the Little Brown Church, the Cardiff Giant and the Spirit Lake Massacre, have already been included in an earlier textbook, *Iowa, the Land Across the River*, published in 1963. They are included here because we felt no book on Iowa would be complete without them.

A word of appreciation is due to the many Iowa editors—men like W. Earl Hall and Ken Berg of the *Mason City Globe-Gazette*, Jackson Baty of the *Osage Press-News*, Wit Ledbetter of the *Nevada Evening Journal*, Charles Anderson of the *Sioux City Sunday Journal* and Dave Elder of the *Washington Evening Journal*—for their help and interest in having a weekly column devoted to Iowa history.

Research for these articles was accompanied by personal interviews whenever possible and great help was always rendered in every way by Miss Helen Aten and the fine staff of the State Traveling Library in Des Moines.

A special note of thanks to the entire staff of the Wallace-Homestead Company for their many efforts in behalf of this and previous books and to Mrs. Velma Adamson of Wallace-Homestead for her help in editing this book.

DON BROWN

Table of Contents

PART ONE   WAY OUT WEST IN IOWAY

1	A Fort in Flames	4
2	Black Hawk, the Fighting Chief	8
3	Chief Mahaska	11
4	The Tegarden Massacre	14
5	Gunsmoke—Iowa Style	17
6	The Death of Homer	20
7	Red Man's Revenge	23
8	The Spirit Lake Massacre	26
9	Here Comes the Railroad!	29

PART TWO   TALES OF CRIME AND MYSTERY

10	White Beans for Hanging	34
11	The Boys From Troublesome Creek	37
12	Davis City's Desperadoes	40
13	Who Stole John Foreman's Calves?	43
14	The Day They Blew Up the Courthouse	46
15	Villisca's Darkest Night	50
16	Buried Gold and Watchful Ghosts	54
17	Hey! That's John Dillinger!	57

PART THREE   FAVORITE STORIES OF HAWKEYELAND

18	Spirit Lake and the City Slicker	62
19	The Vision in the Wildwood	65
20	The Town That Fetes the Hobos	68
21	When the Sun Hid Her Head	71
22	Jumbo on a Rampage	74
23	A Palace of Corn	77
24	The Cardiff Giant	80
25	The U.S.S. Iowa	83

PART FOUR   BRAVE ONES ALL

26	Rescue Mission to Spirit Lake	88
27	Heroes of Harpers Ferry	92
28	The Vote That Saved a President	95
29	Heroine of the Bridge	98
30	The Five Sullivans	100

Part Five   WRITERS, ARTISTS AND DREAMERS

31	The Man Without a Poem	104
32	Iowa's Wild West Writer	110
33	Bob Burdette, Homespun Humorist	112
34	America's Waltz King	114
35	Jack London and Kelly's Army	117
36	American Gothic	120

Part Six   A FEW ASSORTED CHARACTERS

37	Abner Kneeland's Dream Colony	124
38	The Preacher and the Bell	127
39	August Werner's Flying Machine	130
40	When Mrs. Bloomer Came to Iowa	133
41	And Mary Rogan Got Dunked!	136
42	Those Terrible Cherry Sisters!	140

Part Seven   SOME MEN WE CAN'T FORGET

43	Iowa's Frontier Governor	146
44	Idol of the Roaring West	150
45	Jesse Raised an Apple Tree	154
46	Ringling Brothers, Kings of the Circus	157
47	"He Can Touch the Throne of God"	160
48	Into the Wild Blue Yonder!	164
49	When Bryan Came to Iowa	167
50	Billy Sunday, Voice of the Sawdust Trail	170

Index 173

Tell a Tale of Iowa

UNDER HAWKEYE SKIES

Do you ever hear the voices
    as the wind glides over
        the Iowa prairie?
The voices of Indians
    as they search the woods for game?
Of the homesteaders
    as they carved the wilderness
        into farmsteads,
Or of the Mormons
    as they trudged along
        on their Holy March?

Do you ever see the visions
    under Hawkeye Skies?
The vision of Dubuque
    as he mined the land for lead?
Of Black Hawk
    as he led his warriors on,
Or of Kate Shelley
    on hands and knees
        on a wind-swept trestle?

Can't you hear their voices?
Can't you see their visions?
    Look for them—
        Listen for them.
For they lived
    and breathed
        and died—
Under Hawkeye Skies.

—F. M. HARTZELL

PART ONE

Way Out West in Ioway

1

A Fort in Flames

SEPTEMBER 5, 1812, was a hot, fall day that caused life in the Army garrison of Fort Madison to drone on a little slower than usual. Dusk had just started to fall and the men were preparing the evening meal when wild yells suddenly arose. Peering out the high walls the white men could see the shining bodies of howling Winnebago and Sac Indians prancing around the stockade. The fort was under attack.

Ever since Fort Madison, named in honor of President James Madison, had been established just above the Des Moines River rapids three years earlier, the Indians had been a source of trouble. For one thing, the red men felt that all land west of the Father of Waters was theirs and resented the intrusion of the white man and his stockade. The English traders along the Mississippi were partly responsible for this attitude as they did all within their power to stir up the Indians against America.

Until 1812, however, trouble had not been too serious. In fact, much of the time the Indians enjoyed playing tricks on the soldiers. Once they stole the soldiers' firearms while they were working and then gave out with a piercing war whoop. The frightened soldiers ran for their guns and were shocked to find them gone. The Indians laughed and gave the firearms back.

But now they were after blood. Incited by the British, the warriors were out to eliminate the white man's encampment in Indian territory.

The Americans were handicapped by a very poor fighting location. A bluff loomed just behind Fort Madison and deep ravines surrounded it. When Indians attacked they would shoot burning arrows from the bluff and slip up to the walls through the ravines. The fort, which consisted of three blockhouses, a trading place and storehouse, each surrounded by a high fence of pickets, was very hard to defend from the crafty red invaders.

A Fort in Flames

The battle settled down to a long, bitter siege. The first white casualty was Private John Cox who had been caught outside the walls and killed by a tomahawk blow.

When it was completely dark the Indians stopped firing and the weary soldiers waited tensely. But at the break of dawn the Indians came back strong, burning and pillaging the area around. For days the red men continued their relentless attack. Along with his fighting duties, each soldier had to act as a fireman, keeping the roofs of the buildings wet and pulling out the burning arrows.

During one long night of waiting, the commanding officer, Lieutenant Thomas Hamilton, realized the Indians were waiting for a high wind to blow in the direction of the fort before they set fire to the trading post, which was outside the stockade. The sparks would then set the whole post in flames. He quickly formulated a plan that would deprive the savages of that action.

That very night, while the wind was still, Lieutenant Hamilton's men hurled firebrands until the store was a mass of flames. It burned to the ground without endangering the rest of the fort.

Thanks to the bravery of Lieutenant Hamilton and his men, the Indians tired of their invasion and after four days of harassment they left.

Although the immediate danger was past, the Army recognized the vulnerability of Fort Madison and decided its handicap of poor location was a fatal defect. Orders came through from St. Louis and Washington for the men to abandon the fort.

When the orders came, ice was forming on the river making it necessary to postpone the departure until spring. But when the spring of 1813 arrived the government had changed its mind. American generals felt to leave Fort Madison would indicate to the British and the Indians that they had won a moral victory. Also, the Army was planning a northern campaign in which the post would be used as a supply base. So the men settled down to a summer of waiting.

In July the skirmishes started again. First a corporal and three other soldiers were massacred in front of the gate. Then another attack started in which the British furnished the Indians with guns and ammunition.

As the exhausted men fought off the attackers day after day, another danger loomed up. Their supplies of powder, shells and firewood were rapidly being depleted. And worse, their food rations were getting low. Starvation was staring Lieutenant Hamilton and his men in the face.

By September 3, 1813, the twin evils of fatigue and hunger had worn down the loyal band of American soldiers on the frontier outpost. They could see their only course was to escape if they were to avoid death at the hands of the savages. But how to escape? How could dozens of soldiers escape a garrison that was surrounded day and night by Indians?

Once again Lieutenant Hamilton came to the rescue. In the dark of night, after the red men had moved up to the bluff to keep the fort under surveillance, the Americans entered one of the blockhouses. With knives and axes the men toiled until early morning, chipping away earth to form a trench leading to the river.

Then they collected a few possessions and each man, except one, dropped into the trench and sneaked through the still darkness to the river. The man who remained waited until all had reached the river. Then he threw a flaming torch upon the fort and darted through the trench. The other soldiers were waiting in Indian canoes and pushed out into the stream as he leaped aboard.

A moment later the fort was transformed into a glory of dancing flames. The Indians howled with rage as they raced to the river and found the white men on their way to safety.

Fort Madison burned on until all that remained was a large stone chimney. For many years it stood, a symbol of American courage in defense of the first fort in Iowa.

2

Black Hawk, the Fighting Chief

Of ALL the Indians who once roamed the Iowa prairies, the name of Black Hawk stands out like a shining star in a dark sky.

To the white man Black Hawk was a fierce enemy, a war-mongering leader and a desperate fighter.

To the red man he was the bravest of all chiefs, a loyal leader and a great inspiration to all Indians who wanted to preserve their hunting land.

Black Hawk was born in the Sac Indian village of Saukenuk, which was located on the Rock River in Illinois about four miles east from the present city of Davenport. The year was 1767 and Saukenuk was a beautiful, rich village. The Sacs loved their home.

Black Hawk grew up fast. When he was only sixteen he killed his first enemy, an Osage brave. In accordance with Sac custom, Black Hawk was allowed to wear feathers and paint his face from then on. The young brave was only five feet eight inches tall and thin and wiry. He wore his hair and feathers in a shock perched on the back of his head. With his painted face and straight hair, Black Hawk presented a menacing appearance.

The young Black Hawk grew up to hate Americans, as he felt they were attempting to move the Indians off their rich farming and hunting grounds. This hatred resulted in a series of battles in 1832 that have become known as the Black Hawk War.

The background for this war actually started in 1804 when a small delegation of Sacs and Foxes visited St. Louis and signed a treaty giving land east of the Mississippi, including Saukenuk, to the American government for use by the white man.

Black Hawk, who was a minor chief, became incensed when he heard of this. He said he would not recognize the treaty as binding or legal and accused the delegation of being drunk from the white man's liquor

By Elroy Gertner

Black Hawk

when they made the agreement. For over twenty-seven years Black Hawk successfully resisted attempts to move his village.

Meanwhile, the head chiefs of the Sacs, Pashepaho and Keokuk, and Wapello, head chief of the Foxes, moved their tribes of several thousand across the Mississippi near Davenport, Iowa.

Black Hawk and about eight hundred of his followers stayed behind to make trouble for the white settlers. Only after more soldiers started into the area to expel the Indians did Black Hawk move his band across the Mississippi in 1831.

However, the fighting chief was determined to try to regain his village. He went to Keokuk's camp on the Iowa River and while his warriors danced the war dance, Black Hawk made a speech urging Keokuk and his braves to join him in driving out the whites. Keokuk's braves became inflamed by his speech and chanted their approval of his plan.

But then the peaceful Keokuk spoke. He told of the great number of whites and that any fight was doomed to failure for the red man. But, Chief Keokuk declared, he would lead them in their fight if they would first put all of their women and children to death, as they would starve in their absence.

When the warriors heard this they decided to stay at home. From that day on, Black Hawk hated Keokuk.

The persistent Black Hawk did get some braves from other tribes to help him and in the spring of 1832 they crossed the Mississippi. The battle was on!

The white men had more guns, ammunition and the terrible cannon. Both sides were ruthless and many women and children were killed.

The short war ended in August of 1832 at the mouth of the Bad Axe River in Wisconsin when the fleeing Indians were overtaken and many were slaughtered. Black Hawk was defeated.

The old warrior was captured and taken to Prairie du Chien, Wisconsin. From there he was taken to Jefferson Barracks at St. Louis, Missouri. After some time there he was transported on a long trip through the eastern United States to show him the might of America and to display to Easterners a famous Indian chief. In 1833 Black Hawk was released and returned to Iowa.

For a time the elderly chief lived in a cabin near Fort Madison on Devil Creek. He then moved with his wife to new quarters on the Des Moines River near Iowaville.

In his last public words at Fort Madison in 1838, Black Hawk spoke to a large gathering of Indians and whites and said:

I liked my towns, my cornfields, and the home of my people. I fought for it. It is now yours—keep it as we did—it will produce you good crops.

In October of 1838, Black Hawk passed to his reward at the age of seventy-one. He was buried near his Iowaville cabin in a sitting position facing the southeast. In his left hand was a cane given to him by Henry Clay.

Years later Black Hawk's grave was opened and his bones were stolen by a white man. The government recovered the bones and they were placed in a historical museum at Burlington, but a few years later the building was destroyed by fire and the mortal remains of Iowa's fighting Chief Black Hawk were lost.

3

Chief Mahaska

In the warm quiet of a spring evening in 1824, a tall, stately Indian made camp for the night near the mouth of the Des Moines River. His name was Mahaska, or White Cloud in the Indian tongue, and he was chief of the Iowa (sometimes called Ioway) tribe. Mahaska had succeeded his father, Mauhawgaw, as chief after his father was slain by a band of Sioux. Immediately Mahaska proved his worth by leading a war party against the Sioux and coming back with the scalp of the offending chief.

Although a fighting chief, this evening Mahaska was not concerned with battles. He was on the first leg of a long and important journey. With other members of his race, Mahaska was traveling to Washington, D. C., to see the leader of the white men, President James Monroe. The Indians were going to see for themselves how mighty these white creatures were and how they lived.

Mahaska sat before the fire, roasting a piece of venison, when he heard someone approaching. Quickly he reached for his tomahawk, fearful of the dreaded Sioux. To his surprise a beautiful Indian woman stepped from the brush before the campfire. It was Mahaska's wife, Rantchewaime, who had been left at home in their village of Iowaville, near the present site of Eldon.

Rantchewaime, known as Female Flying Pigeon, explained that she wanted to go to see the White Father too and begged Mahaska to let her accompany him. Because she was Mahaska's favorite of his seven wives, he reluctantly said she could go.

The next day they started off together and met the remainder of the party. There were nineteen chiefs, four women, six interpreters and a few white men who were to show them around.

The red men were amazed by the many things they saw in Washington and the whites were curious to see these Indians from the West.

They were especially attracted by the great beauty and intelligence of Rantchewaime. She was so different from the savages they had heard so much about.

Although it is not known if Rantchewaime met President Monroe, as her husband did, she charmed many officials. General Hughes, an Indian agent, spoke highly of the Indian woman and her portrait was painted by an artist at the capital. For many years it hung in his studio.

When Mahaska and Rantchewaime ended their visit and returned to their Iowa village they both carried a new outlook on life. Mahaska sold some of the tribe's Missouri land holdings to the government and received an income of $500 each year for ten years. His tribe was also to receive tools and cattle, for their chief had promised President Monroe that from now on the Iowas would live in peace.

Rantchewaime busied herself spreading the word to other Indian women of the wonderful homes and cooking utensils the white women had.

A few months after their return from Washington, Rantchewaime and Mahaska were riding horseback across the prairie. Rantchewaime was holding their four-year-old son before her on her pony. Mahaska was riding ahead to scout for enemy tribes when he noticed his wife was not behind him. Backtracking, he found the pony munching grass and the little boy sitting beside it. Rantchewaime was lying still upon the ground. "Mother is asleep," the boy said, but the grief-stricken chief realized she had been killed by a fall from her horse.

The funeral for Mahaska's beautiful wife was an impressive affair. All of the presents given to her by the white people were put in a box with her body. Then the makeshift coffin was placed on a high platform to bring her as near to the Great Spirit as possible.

Mahaska killed a dog and the warriors were called for a feast. Then he killed another dog and a horse and left their bodies near the platform. The horse was to carry Rantchewaime to the Spirit Land and the dog was to hunt deer for her.

Rantchewaime was a kind and generous person. Her death caused great sorrow for Mahaska and for his people.

In 1833 the son of a subordinate Iowa chief was killed by the Omaha Indians. Although his tribe wanted revenge, Mahaska would not allow

CHIEF MAHASKA 13

Rantchewaime

Mahaska

them to go on the warpath. He had promised the White Father in Washington that his tribe would live in peace and he intended to keep that promise.

However, some of his warriors went into the Omaha lands in western Iowa and returned with the scalps of six Omahas. When this news reached St. Louis, General Clarke ordered General Hughes to arrest the Iowa braves. Mahaska surrendered the guilty men to the Army officers because they had disobeyed his orders and violated the white man's law.

Two of the murderers escaped from imprisonment at Fort Leavenworth and thirsted for revenge against their chief. They learned Mahaska was camped on the Nodaway River and set out to find him. They reached the camp at midnight and shot Chief Mahaska while he was sleeping in his tepee.

The two assassins escaped but one was later killed by a member of the Iowa tribe. The other sought refuge among the Otoes but when they learned of his cowardly deed they executed him.

Mahaska's proud name now designates a county in the Des Moines River valley, part of our state which the once-powerful tribe ruled.

4

The Tegarden Massacre

EVERYONE knows the story of the terrible Spirit Lake massacre but few are familiar with Iowa's other Indian killing, the Tegarden massacre. This took place in 1843, fourteen years before the Spirit Lake tragedy and occurred in another part of the state. While only three whites were killed and two seriously wounded, compared with the thirty-two dead at Spirit Lake, the episode is dramatic evidence of some of the danger early settlers faced in the Iowa Territory.

Actually, Mose Tegarden brought most of the trouble on himself. During the winter of 1842-43, he and his partner, a shady character named Atwood, moved to a new cabin in Fayette County in northeastern Iowa. Tegarden brought with him his wife and three children—a boy, nine, a girl, seven, and a three-year-old baby.

The men supplemented their existence of scratching out a living on the prairie by selling whiskey to the Indians. This practice was contrary to federal law but the two men found it profitable enough to warrant a little risk.

One bleak morning a Winnebago from the tribe of "Little Hill" left his gun in pawn with Tegarden and Atwood for some rum. Then Tegarden sold the weapon to another settler at a nice profit.

When the red man returned for his gun he was upset and angry because the traders had sold it. Atwood and Tegarden smoothed over the matter and talked the Winnebago into accepting more firewater for the traded gun. Everything seemed to be settled.

It was an unusually cold March 25, 1843, when the same Indian and two companions appeared at the Tegarden cabin. They were loud and threatening and demanded more liquor. They also complained about the gun and said the white men were cheaters.

Atwood, in an attempt to pacify them, invited the red men into the cabin and offered them all drinks. Then he and Tegarden started drink-

The Tegarden Massacre 15

ing too. Before long the three Indians and two white men were all drunk.

As the day faded into early darkness, Mrs. Tegarden, a sensible woman who did not approve of her husband's illegal activities, became fearful of the lengthy presence of the Indians. The more they drank the louder they talked and the more unruly they became. She decided to take the children and leave.

As the woman started bundling up the children to make the mile journey to the neighbors, her drunken husband saw what she was doing and would not allow them to go. Later Mrs. Tegarden managed to slip away but her children remained.

By midnight the youngsters were asleep and the white men were dozing in a drunken stupor. But the three Indians were awake.

They quietly arose from their pretended slumber and tied up the surprised Tegarden and Atwood. Then they tortured Atwood for half an hour before killing him. His frantic yells and pleading screams delighted the Winnebagos.

When Atwood died they started on Tegarden. The trader, now shocked to his senses, begged the savages that if they intended to kill him to do so at once without prolonging the pain. They considered his request and politely complied by taking a gun and blasting him in the head.

The ruthless Winnebagos next killed the baby and tomahawked the boy, leaving him seriously injured but still alive. One Indian beat the little girl in her bed with his tomahawk. But in watching the murderous events in the cabin the girl had noticed that as soon as the victim was dead the Indians left him alone. So, dazed and bleeding, she lay very still and pretended to be dead. The Indian left.

Surveying the bloody scene, the killers decided their revenge for the gun deal had been sufficiently spent and went outside to a shed to gather their ponies. Later they returned and set fire to the tiny cabin. In the red glow of the burning structure the Winnebagos rode away over the snow-laden prairie.

Federal authorities later caught up with the murderers and jailed them in Dubuque. Each man was tried separately, each on a different day with a different judge. All were found guilty and sentenced to hang. History does not indicate whether or not this punishment was ever carried out.

But what about the children? When the Indians went to get their ponies the terribly wounded boy and girl escaped and stumbled along the path until they reached the neighbor's cabin and safety.

Both recovered from their wounds but it is said that for the rest of her life the girl carried a deep scar on her face—a tragic reminder of Iowa's Tegarden massacre.

5

Gunsmoke—Iowa Style

WOODBURY MASSEY was generally considered one of the finest, cleanest young men in the little mining settlement of Dubuque. He was the eldest of an orphaned family of several brothers and sisters, and had served as a father to them. That's why the little town seethed with anger one day in 1835 when young Woodbury Massey was murdered.

The story, as the people in town talked it over, was this: Young Massey had brought his brothers and sister into the lead mining region to seek his fortune. After he had made his claim, a father and son by the name of Smith laid claim to the same mine. The Smiths were described as "evil and treacherous men."

Woodbury, being a peaceful fellow, took the dispute before a local magistrate and it was decided that the property rightfully belonged to Massey. Shortly after the issue was settled, the young man and the sheriff went to put the Smiths off the land. Just as Massey stepped on the property, the Smiths, who had been waiting in ambush, rose and fired, killing Woodbury instantly. This murder occurred in sight of Massey's own home and his brothers and sister saw him fall dead.

As word of the atrocity flashed through the settlement a posse was formed and set out after the Smiths. They were soon captured and taken to what is now Mineral Point, Wisconsin, to stand trial. A clever lawyer pointed out the crime was committed across the Mississippi and therefore a court outside that territory had no right to sentence the two men. They were released but were given a definite warning from the townspeople of Dubuque and Galena, Illinois, where one of the Massey brothers lived, never again to come to either town. Woodbury Massey's brokenhearted family resumed their life on their mine and did the best they could.

Then, several months later, the Massey boy who lived in Galena was shocked to see the elder Smith walking down the street. Here was his brother's killer right before him! In a moment of wild emotion the avenging brother overtook Smith and shot him dead. Since the townspeople all sympathized with Massey and thought Smith's demise was somewhat of a blessing, young Massey was never arrested or tried.

Now the score was even; one dead Massey, one dead Smith. If left to stand this way the story might be ended, but the younger Smith was now thirsting for revenge. He returned to Dubuque, visited the local saloon and told everyone who would listen that he was out to "get" one or the other of the Massey brothers.

This threat soon reached the ears of Louisa Massey, the young sister, and struck terror into her heart. She had worshipped her elder brother and his death had hurt her deeply. Now this evil man was boasting that he would kill another brother. She knew Smith had a bad temper and was a crack shot. Something must be done!

Louisa decided that her brothers were no match for Smith so it was up to her to save them. She dug out a large sunbonnet that covered her fair hair and shadowed her features and slipped a gun away from her brother while he was sleeping. Since she did not know Smith by sight, Louisa got a young boy to accompany her and point him out. Then the innocent-looking pair—a young girl in a sunbonnet and a little boy—started down the dusty street.

They found Smith standing with some men in front of the general store. "There he is," the boy whispered. Louisa's heart skipped as she saw Smith's six-shooter at his side. But the girl did not hesitate. She knew what must be done.

Deliberately she stalked up to Smith and in a voice trembling with anger said, "If you are Smith, defend yourself!"

The man made a motion toward his gun but he was too late. Holding her pistol firmly with both hands, Louisa squeezed the trigger and sent a blast straight at the bad man's heart. With a cry Smith reeled back and fell to the street. Because a wallet carried in his breast pocket deflected the bullet, Smith was not killed but was seriously wounded.

Louisa and the boy turned and ran homeward. She spent the night at the home of the town grocer and left the next morning to stay with relatives in Illinois. A few years later she was married there.

Although Louisa Massey was legally a fugitive from justice, no attempt was ever made to arrest her. In fact, most people were thrilled by her bravery. In 1836, the legislature of the Wisconsin Territory, in which Iowa was then included, named an eastern Iowa county "Louisa" in honor of the young girl who had routed a murderer and saved the lives of her brothers.

6

The Death of Homer

Today Homer, Iowa, is just a wide place in the road with a feeling of yesteryear about it. It sleeps on the prairie while a frantic world rushes by. The few dilapidated buildings and sagging homes are testimony of another age.

But it was not always like this. There was a time when Homer was a proud town. It was the county seat of Webster County, had a busy land office and boasted many stores and professional men. Then its bubble broke and once-proud Homer suffered misfortune after misfortune and even became a loser in a wrestling match between two of Webster County's most prominent men.

Webster County was established by the state legislature in 1853 and Homer was designated as the county seat. Cabins were built, a school was started and the little town began to hum.

The land around the area was rich and attracted many settlers who homesteaded it for $1.25 an acre. To meet the demand a federal land office was located in the village, causing settlers to tramp into town from miles around. Many pioneers coming from the East stopped in Des Moines and were told to travel on to Homer to settle.

One newcomer wrote: *Coming out of the prairie west of the timber we saw a sight never to be forgotten—land covered with a luxuriant growth of grass, known as "blue stem." It grew tall as a man could reach. I said to the boys "this is good enough for me." We had our pick of the land, as it all belonged to Uncle Sam and he only wanted $1.25 an acre for it.*

By 1855 Homer was a boom town. The firm of Snell and Butterworth started a wholesale store in Homer, purchased and sold real estate, built a mill and grew wealthy serving the settlers. There was even talk around town for a new brickyard, a wholesale grocery and other new businesses.

Then a rumble of trouble could be heard around the county. Fort Dodge, about twenty miles to the north, was suddenly enjoying a revival of prosperity. It had been practically abandoned in 1853 but then started to grow. Fort Dodge was fortunate in having some energetic boosters who worked night and day for their town's growth.

Without warning the land office was moved to Fort Dodge. Many Homer citizens followed it, shocking the city fathers into realizing that here was a new rival!

As the rivalry and competition built up, Fort Dodge announced a campaign to move the county seat from Homer to their city.

The residents of Homer were not only surprised by this fantastic idea, they were outraged. But they didn't think Fort Dodge would be able to convince the voters of Webster County of such a preposterous idea. However, the Homerites did not reckon with the good people of Newcastle.

Newcastle was a small settlement about ten miles northeast of Homer. It was so small that nobody paid much attention to it. And it wouldn't have been of much importance except for the fact that Newcastle joined Fort Dodge in the election and the voters decided to move their governmental seat away from Homer to Fort Dodge. The death knell had started to toll.

Feeling ran high after the election with charges and counter charges on both sides. A well-known incident occurred when John Maxwell, a lawyer from Homer, accused Fort Dodge backers of fraudulent practices in the election.

After hearing this, John F. Duncombe, one of Fort Dodge and northern Iowa's most important men, challenged Maxwell to wrestle it out.

The details of this match seem to be lost to history but Duncombe was the winner. Maxwell, defeated and disgusted, "spit on his fire, called his dog" and moved away. Duncombe lived to see his town become one of the leading cities in the state.

What about Homer? It struggled along in defeat, dying a little every day. To add insult to injury, Hamilton County was formed and included Homer but it was never even considered for the county seat. Instead that honor went to Newcastle, which prospered and grew into the present city of Webster City.

The final death blow came when the railroad went through Webster City and Fort Dodge leaving Homer stranded.

Poor Homer! It had been outvoted, outfought and outsmarted. Now it stands quiet and alone without even a glimmer of hope that it might ever again be called the most promising town in Iowa.

7

Red Man's Revenge

THERE's a grave on a hill overlooking the Des Moines River in Boone County with quite a story behind it. A monument that stands nearby informs the passerby:

MILTON LOTT

> Died December 18, 1846, from freezing
> while escaping from the Sioux Indians.
> Aged twelve years. This was the first
> death in Boone County.

But what this inscription fails to tell is that this lonely grave is thought by some historians to be the first link in a chain of events that resulted in one of Iowa's most terrible tragedies.

In the summer of 1846, a trapper and trader named Henry Lott settled in Boone County. With him were his wife and two sons.

But Lott did not confine his activities to trapping alone. He found more profit in selling whiskey to the Indians by day and stealing their horses by night.

One of the tribes that roamed the area and often traded with Lott was a band of renegade Sioux led by a fierce chieftain named Sidominadota.

In the fall of 1846, the Indians lost several horses and a little investigation showed them to be tied in the woods near Lott's cabin. Although Lott denied stealing the horses, the Indians did not believe him.

Sidominadota was outraged and ordered Lott and his family to get out of the country. When he refused, the Indians left telling Lott he had "one moon" in which to leave or he would suffer at their hands.

In December the Indians returned and broke into the cabin. They found only Mrs. Lott and her twelve-year-old son, Milton. The father and another son were away. The intruders pushed Milton outside and told him to round up all of his father's horses and bring them to the cabin. If he did not, they said, they would kill his mother.

The winter storms had set in and the day was bitterly cold. Milton, although he had no jacket or coat, knew that the only way he could save his mother was to go for help. He made for the river which was frozen over and started downstream to a settlement called Pea's Point, near the present town of Boone.

Meanwhile Lott and the other boy had returned and saw the Indians around the cabin. Realizing the danger of the situation and the number of red men, father and son also started off to Pea's Point for help. They went through the woods, rather than down the river, and did not know the younger boy was also on the way.

Mile after mile the weary Milton trotted along on the ice. Hours went by and still the boy forged on through the bitter cold. The sun was now down and the cold wind seemed to cut through his body.

Finally, when he was to the point of exhaustion and his limbs were so numb they would no longer act at his command, the boy fell into a featherbed of snow. He closed his eyes and relaxed as sleep crept over him. His mission was forgotten.

Henry Lott and his older son reached the settlement and told their tale of terror. A rescue expedition was quickly organized and sent out.

Returning to the cabin the rescuers found that Sidominadota and his band were gone; the cabin ransacked, cattle dead and the horses missing. Mrs. Lott was alone, hysterical with fright and worry. Despite her distraught condition she managed to tell them that Milton must have gone for help.

A detail was sent to the river bank where they soon discovered the boy's footprints in the deep snow. As the men followed the tracks down the river they marveled at the lad's endurance. For over twenty miles they traced the route of the heroic boy. Then the trail came to an end. Milton's frozen body was found where he had fallen.

After encasing his son's body in a hollow log for later burial, Lott returned to his cabin and tended his wife. But her ordeal had been too great and she died a few weeks later. With both his wife and son gone, Lott swore revenge against Sidominadota.

Lott, who later remarried, and his son left Boone County and settled in Humboldt County. Always keeping his eyes open for a clue to the whereabouts of Sidominadota, the trader heard in 1854 that the Indian was camped nearby.

Lott and his son went to the Indian village. Hiding in the thick brush, they saw the hated Sioux leader. Later they ambushed the chieftain and killed him. After Sidominadota was out of the way, the Lotts brutally killed his aged mother, wife and children. It is said that someone later took Sidominadota's skull to Homer, then county seat of Webster County, and impaled it on a post where it remained for some time.

After completing their gory mission and plundering the camp, Lott and his family escaped to California. Reports say he died there a few years later at the hands of a lynching party for a crime he had committed.

But the story doesn't end here. For Sidominadota's brother took over leadership of the Sioux outlaws and vowed he would avenge the slaughter of his brother and mother.

This brother was Inkpaduta, ". . . a savage monster in human shape, fitted only for the darkest corner of Hades." Three years later, in March, 1857, Inkpaduta carried out his oath with the hideous killing of thirty-two people in the Lake Okoboji area in the infamous Spirit Lake massacre.

So that's why a tale of violence, revenge and Iowa's terrible Indian massacre can all be traced back to the grave of young Milton Lott, sleeping peacefully along the river bluffs in Boone County.

(Author's Note: Some historians discount the Lott incident as having a direct influence on the Spirit Lake Massacre. Thomas Teakle in his book *The Spirit Lake Massacre*, published by the State Historical Society in 1918, discounts this theory and does not believe Inkpaduta and Sidominadota were related. *History of Boone County*, published in 1880, states the two Indians were cousins. However, one of the most respected historians, Benjamin F. Gue, in his *History of Iowa* (1904, four volumes), details the Lott story and supports the theory that the two men were brothers and that Sidominadota's slaying was *one* of the major factors precipitating the Spirit Lake tragedy.)

8

The Spirit Lake Massacre

Breakfast was on the table in Rowland Gardner's cabin on the cold, clear morning of March 8, 1857.

Gardner's cabin was a snug log structure located on the south shore of West Okoboji. Besides Gardner and his wife, the family consisted of thirteen-year-old Abigail, a small son, their married daughter, Mrs. Luce, her husband and the Luces' two children.

Suddenly the latch of the door was lifted and an Indian stood before the startled family. He demanded food, which they immediately provided. As the brave was eating, fourteen other Indians crowded their way into the small cabin. Among this group was Inkpaduta, chief of the little band of renegade Indians. Inkpaduta, or Scarlet Point, as he was often called, was a savage man over six feet tall with face pitted and scarred from smallpox. He was feared not only by the whites but by other Indians as well.

The Indians ate the food provided for them by Mrs. Gardner and then demanded ammunition and guns. When one brave tried to take a powder horn from the wall, Harvey Luce, the son-in-law, interfered and one of the Indians threatened him with a gun.

Finally the Indians left but Mr. Gardner knew that their actions meant trouble ahead. The men felt the settlers that lived in the little cabins around the lakes should be warned about Inkpaduta and his men.

Therefore, about two o'clock that afternoon, Luce and another man set out in the cold to spread the alarm. Meanwhile, Gardner remained with the family—his gun ready and the door barred.

An hour after the men left, the sound of shots echoed through the stillness. The Indians had ambushed and killed both men.

Two hours later, Gardner opened the cabin door and stepped out to look around. The setting sun cast a crimson glow on the snow and

THE SPIRIT LAKE MASSACRE 27

Gue, "History of Iowa"

An Old Painting of Abbie Gardner Being Taken Prisoner

frozen lakes. The air was still with a sense of foreboding hanging low overhead.

Suddenly Gardner saw figures approaching his cabin. "They're coming back," he cried, and ran inside the shelter.

Mr. Gardner wanted to bar the door and fight to the last but his wife convinced him he should admit the Indians and try to be friendly with them.

Gardner unlocked the door and nine savages roughly pushed their way over the threshold and called for a meal. But as Rowland Gardner turned to get flour from the bin he was shot in the back without warning. Iowa's terrible massacre had begun.

The women were ruthlessly pushed out of the cabin into the snow. Then the Indians smashed their skulls with gun-butts. The three smaller children were clinging to Abigail but the fierce red men dragged and pulled them from her one by one and killed them with pieces of stove wood.

Before Abigail's terrified eyes, the Indians scalped the bodies of her family. Later that night she looked on in horror as the savages danced around a fire, singing their weird chants and holding long poles from which dangled the scalps of her murdered family. However, the Indians did not kill Abigail but took her captive instead.

In the next few days Inkpaduta and his tribe ravaged around the lake region killing thirty-two innocent men, women and children. When they finished, the Indians stripped bark from a tree, drew illustrations of their terrible deeds and left it as a monument. Besides Abigail Gardner, the Indians captured Mrs. J. M. Thatcher, Mrs. Margaret Marble and Mrs. Lydia Noble.

Inkpaduta knew word of the massacre would soon be spread to the garrison at Fort Dodge so he and his band started for South Dakota.

Along the way Mrs. Thatcher became too ill to travel so she was thrown into the Big Sioux River from a narrow bridge. As she tried to swim, the Indians clubbed and shot her. Mrs. Noble was also killed by Inkpaduta's son, Roaring Cloud, when her weeping bothered him.

The Indians kept both Mrs. Marble and Abigail Gardner captive as they traveled from place to place. Late the following summer they were both traded to an Indian agent at Yellow Medicine River in Minnesota. The price the agent paid for Abigail was two horses, twelve blankets, two kegs of powder, twenty pounds of tobacco, thirty-two yards of blue cloth and thirty-seven and one-half yards of calico and ribbon. After months of terror and hardship, thirteen-year-old Abigail Gardner was free. However, Inkpaduta was never captured and punished for his terrible deeds.

Years later Abigail Gardner, now Mrs. Sharpe, returned to the site of the killings, restored the family cabin and lived in it. She wrote a book telling of the Indian massacre and her horrible experiences connected with it.

Today a monument stands by the restored Gardner cabin. It serves as a reminder of Iowa's worst Indian attack and the quiet courage of a thirteen-year-old girl.

(For an exciting sequel to the Spirit Lake tragedy, see Chapter 26, "Rescue Mission to Spirit Lake.")

9

Here Comes the Railroad!

Courtesy, State Department of History and Archives
An Early Train

It was a big day in frontier Iowa when the sound of men laying railroad tracks drifted over the prairie. And it was an even bigger day when the high "Iron Horse" finally made its arrival in a town.

For many years early Iowans had dreamed of the day when their town would be linked by a railroad with the great markets in Chicago. As early as 1836 one John Plumbe, Jr., of Dubuque, talked about building a railroad. By the middle of the last century many projects, schemes and charters were announced for railroad construction. Most of these never materialized.

One of the first projects in railroad construction started in 1854 as the brainchild of a shady slicker from New York named H. P. Adams. Adams, who was said to be a fugitive from justice, proposed a line that was to start at Lyons (now a part of Clinton) and run westward through Fort Des Moines and then on to Council Bluffs. Adams' project was called the Lyons-Iowa Central Railroad Company.

Hundreds of men, many of whom were immigrants, were put to work building grades and cutting timber for ties. Excitement ran throughout eastern Iowa as word of the railroad spread.

To finance the line, Adams received money by subscription from businessmen along the route of the road and even persuaded a number of counties to vote bonds.

The whole project collapsed when Adams absconded with a great deal of the cash and left the counties with taxes to pay, the laborers with no work and no money and, of course, no railroad.

The Lyons-Iowa Central line was called the "Calico Road" because the laborers were paid in groceries and drygoods, including large quantities of calico.

Despite the failure of the Calico Road, other companies were making progress in getting the Iron Horse to Iowa. The first line in the state extended west from Davenport to Iowa City with a branch line from Wilton south to Muscatine. The first passenger train ran from Davenport to Wilton in 1855.

The arrival on July 19, 1855, of Iowa's first locomotive caused a great deal of curiosity on the part of Davenport's citizens. The huge engine, called the "Antoine Le Claire" after Davenport's most prominent resident, had been brought by flatboat across the Mississippi.

Filled with water and fueled with pine from a local sawmill, the "Antoine Le Claire" made its first run loaded with gleeful passengers.

The engineer of the locomotive spotted a large group of Indians eyeing the strange machine with wonder. He waved to the red men to join in on the ride and they, ". . . cast to the winds their blankets, all they had on earth perhaps, and ran with all possible speed down the hill to the track where the Antoine Le Claire stood gently steaming, with shouts and laughter. They swarmed upon and over her, a score of them; and so, with all the passengers, red and white, that could be stuck on the tender and the cab, the first run in this section of the United States was made."

What was probably the first runaway caused by a train in Iowa occurred on this trial run. A team hitched to a Mr. Kincaide's buggy bolted at the sound of the engine and the occupants had to leap out before the buggy was tumbled into a ditch.

Carried away by enthusiasm for the first railroad, the editor of the *Davenport Gazette* looked into the future and wrote:

Here Comes the Railroad!

Who shall contemplate its destiny? Will Cedar River bound its westward labor? Will Iowa City stay its course? Will the great Missouri say, here shall the proud course be stayed? Shall the towering ramparts of the Rocky Mountains give limits to its onward course? No, the quiet shores of the mighty Pacific shall be awakened by the shrill whistle of its engine—the welcome tones of its alarm bell.

Railroad construction continued in the Hawkeye state until the first train pulled into the capital, Iowa City, on January 3, 1856, and was met by thunderous applause and cheers.

Nine years later the Iron Horse reached Des Moines and the following year, 1866, a line extended to Council Bluffs.

Slowly but surely a new dawn of travel was emerging on the Iowa horizon.

PART TWO

Tales of Crime and Mystery

10

White Beans for Hanging

WHEN William Brown first came to Bellevue, in Jackson County, in the 1830's, he was immediately popular with everyone. His pleasing manner and kindly ways combined with his tall, handsome bearing to attract people to him. Brown prospered in the town and soon owned a hotel, general store and meat market. His customers and fellow businessmen all agreed that William Brown was a fine addition to tiny Bellevue.

Then a number of strange characters drifted into Bellevue to work for Brown and a series of events occurred that seemed to indicate the genial newcomer was a little less the gentleman he had first appeared to be.

Not long after the assorted collection of toughs came to work for Brown the crime rate in Jackson County started to soar. Counterfeit money began to appear, horses and cattle were stolen and people were robbed on lonely roadways. Much as the town liked Brown and his gentle little wife, many folks suspected there was a connection between the incidents of crime and the gang the friendly hotelman had imported into town.

Soon Bellevue acquired a reputation as a lawless area. Some citizens moved away and others started carrying firearms at all times. Something had to be done.

Something was done on the night of January 8, 1839, when James Mitchell's cabin was broken into and robbed. Mitchell was at a big dance in town when word came of the robbery. Furious, he stalked from the dance floor to search for the thieves. Someone told him that James Thompson, one of Brown's gang, was responsible. The angry Mitchell found Thompson and, in the fight that resulted, shot and killed the outlaw.

When Mitchell returned to the dance and told what he had done the townsfolk panicked. The dance broke up with the dancers all fleeing to their homes to be safe from the vengeful mob Brown would surely raise.

Then Sheriff Warren and some deputies arrived in town and quieted the residents. The sheriff promised that justice would be done to Mitchell, but Brown and his henchmen would not be allowed to interfere. For safekeeping the officer stationed his deputies around Mitchell's house. This was done mainly to protect Mitchell from Brown's men. There was no jail in Bellevue. Rumors circulated that the outlaws intended to blow up the house with a charge of gunpowder.

Meantime Sheriff Warren decided it was time to rid Bellevue of the Brown plague. He went to Judge Wilson in Dubuque and got a warrant for the arrest of Brown and his entire gang.

A force of around forty men was formed to help arrest the Bellevue gang. Many of these volunteers had served in the Black Hawk War and knew what it was to face danger. When they approached the hotel they saw a red flag floating over it with the words "Victory or Death." This was not going to be an easy arrest.

The showdown came in front of the hotel as the town waited breathlessly behind cover. The ringleader met the posse at the door with drawn guns.

"What do you intend to do?" he demanded.

"Arrest you all," replied the sheriff.

Brown lowered his gun but it discharged and narrowly missed one of the sheriff's men. Both sides then opened fire as they darted for cover. Brown was the first to be hit and was killed instantly. The sheriff's men stormed the hotel and rounded up the rest of the culprits. That night there was peace in Bellevue but there was also sorrow for four citizens had been killed in the fighting and several others were wounded.

The next morning thirteen prisoners sat before the judgment of a jury composed of eighty men. The outlaws pleaded for mercy while Anson Harrington, a respected citizen, argued for immediate hanging. The judge ordered a poll of the jury.

Then one of the strangest scenes ever enacted in Iowa took place.

Two men, one with a box containing red and white beans, the other with an empty box, passed among the jury. The man carrying the beans aid:

"White beans for hanging, colored beans for whipping."

The juryman then chose his color of bean and dropped it into the empty box.

"White beans for hanging, colored beans for whipping," and another man voted.

And so they passed until all eighty had cast their votes. The judge totaled the result.

"The prisoners will arise and hear the verdict," he directed. The trembling men stood.

"By a margin of three colored beans the jury has decided upon whipping."

Each prisoner was then lashed upon his bare back, the number of lashes determined by his past record. The former desperadoes were then placed in boats on the Mississippi with rations for three days and sent away from Iowa soil.

(Author's Note: This punishment did not deter several members of the gang from pursuing long and active careers in crime, however. Six of the old Brown gang were involved in 1854 in the murder and robbery of Colonel George Davenport in his Rock Island home. Three of the culprits were executed and one died in prison.)

11

The Boys From Troublesome Creek

At about the same time that the James boys were making a name for themselves in Missouri during the 1870's, western Iowa was troubled with a gang of roughnecks aptly called the "Troublesome Gang." It was so named because they lived near Troublesome Creek in the southeastern part of Audubon County.

At first the gang's principal activities seem to have been hard drinking and horse racing. But they soon grew bolder and started stealing stock, grain and personal property from their neighbors. Before long their maraudings extended into Cass, Adair and Shelby Counties.

The outlaws' victims were often afraid to report them. Those who dared to arouse the ire of the gang usually would suffer unfortunate consequences, such as buildings mysteriously burning to the ground and cattle dying in fields.

Many Audubon County residents believed the Troublesome Boys had a tie-up with Jesse James and were involved with Jesse in the holdup of a Rock Island passenger train near Adair.

One day some of the troublemakers went to Exira, near Audubon, to spend the afternoon in drinking, fighting, and shooting up the town. After their fun was over and they prepared to leave town that evening, a group of citizens were standing on the walk near the street.

Suddenly one of the outlaws turned and fired a shotgun charge in the direction of the onlookers, causing them to scatter for cover. As they did, the sharp crack of a revolver echoed through the dusty streets and one of the gang fell dead. The rest beat a hasty path into the night.

No one knew who fired the fatal shot, but the Troublesome Boys thought a young man named Hallock, who was quite a sharpshooter, was responsible.

A few days later young Hallock was on his uncle's farm putting corn in the feed bunks when three heavily armed men rode into the lot. He immediately recognized the riders as part of the gang and ran behind a shed. Without hesitating, Hallock opened fire, shooting two of the men from their horses and winging the third as he escaped.

A coroner's jury investigated the shooting and cleared the young sharpshooter with a verdict of "justifiable homicide."

The gang's prestige was diminished by the licking given them by Hallock, but the end of their activities really came when they made the mistake of trying to take on the good people of the little Cass County town of Wiota.

The Troublesome Boys were liquored up when they made their plans and word got out of the impending raid. Immediately, the Wiota townspeople assembled all available men and guns in strategic places.

When the raiding outlaws galloped into town, shooting and cursing, they were met with a hail of bullets that laid low two of the men and scared the tar out of the rest. The Troublesome Gang never again bothered western Iowa.

The story goes that the day following the shooting the father of one of the dead outlaws was taking his son's body home in a lumber wagon when he stopped to chat with some men by the road.

One of the men, in an awkward attempt to make conversation, said to the father, "It must be hard to take a son home under these conditions."

"Well," the old man replied, "Mother and I will now know where he is at night."

Another story of Iowa's wilder days is the lynching that occurred near Harlan.

A young man was caught and his companion killed by a posse in "Buck's Grove," in Shelby County, after they had murdered a Marne, Iowa, man. A crowd of around five hundred gathered at the edge of the woods after the capture and demanded a hanging. A rope was placed around the fugitive's neck and he was taken to a large bridge for the execution.

Just then Sheriff Rainbow of Shelby County rode up and talked to the crowd, asking that the boy be allowed to stand trial and let the law take its course.

Seeing the mood of the mob and the futility of reason, Sheriff Rainbow decided to outsmart them. He stood on a wagon in the middle of the bridge and announced he would take a vote. All those who were for hanging were to gather at the east end of the bridge; those against, at the west.

Then, as the crowd moved to the east to vote for lynching, the sheriff lashed the horses into action and, with the frightened youth, took off in the opposite direction and safely beat the crowd to Harlan. Here the prisoner was lodged in the county jail.

However, the sheriff's quick thinking was to no avail. Late that night a chanting mob stormed the jail and carried the struggling youth to a nearby woods. There, in the eerie light of a full moon, the boy was strung up to the limb of an old oak tree.

In the eyes of frontier Iowa, justice had been rendered and a wrong avenged—all at the end of a length of rope.

12

Davis City's Desperadoes

THERE were six of the Mercer brothers in all and just about everyone in Decatur County in the 1880's agreed that this was six too many.

The Mercer boys, Valentine, Hiram, Henry, Ephram and Sherman, lived with their parents about two miles northwest of Davis City, in southern Decatur County near the Missouri border. Another Mercer, Canada, lived near Ozark, Missouri.

The brothers, particularly Valentine and Hiram, were the local roughnecks. If there was a tavern fight or a street brawl within ten miles in any direction of Davis City, the odds were pretty good that at least one of the Mercer clan was involved.

The troublemakers liked to think of themselves as sort of a second James gang, but they were far from it. Their gains were too puny to bring them much fame as successful bandits. But nobody can deny they were tough. After all, who but a Mercer would shoot up a whole town, rile up peace officers in two states and give their lives in a frantic, last ditch fight over a debt of $1.80?

The saga of the Mercer brothers started in November of 1881 when Valentine and Hiram got one of their infrequent jobs of cutting corn for farmer Frank Taylor. The boys started off early one cool, crisp morning and their work progressed nicely.

But before many hours had passed they wearied of the task and decided there must be an easier way to make a living. So they told Taylor they were quitting and wanted their money.

"How much you 'low I owe you?" the farmer asked.

Valentine replied that they cut sixty shocks at three cents a shock, making a total of $1.80.

"Boys," said Taylor, "when you tie your shocks, I'll pay you. But not until."

Thus began an argument that ended with the farmer not paying the boys anything and they stalked off the property, muttering oaths and swearing they would "get even" with Taylor.

The following day they got their revenge. Hiram enlisted the aid of Ephram, went back to Taylor's place and beat the tar out of the unlucky farmer. Now the score was settled.

A cold wind was whistling down Davis City's main street on November 16, 1881. But City Marshal R. D. R. Topliff wasn't a bit cold. In fact, he was hot and perspiring as he set forth to carry out an official duty. It was a mean job ahead of him too, because he carried a warrant for the arrest of Hiram Mercer for assault.

The marshal, a small, wiry man, deputized R. A. Ford and John Enloe to help bring Mercer in. They found the wanted man in the poolroom.

"Hiram, I got to take you in," the marshal ordered.

"All right," was all Mercer said as he accompanied the lawmen out to the front of the store.

As he passed Valentine, lounging at one of the tables, Hiram whispered, "I'm being arrested, Valentine." The brother followed the men outside.

They were almost to the drugstore when the trouble started. Hiram suddenly bolted and tried to run away but was brought down with a flying tackle from the marshal. The two men struggled fiercely on the ground. Valentine came running into the melee, pulled his gun and shot Deputy Enloe, killing him instantly. Townspeople were now pouring into the street but Valentine held them at bay with wild shots. Then he fired and hit Marshal Topliff in the arm.

Despite the disadvantage of his size, the officer was a gritty man and clung to Hiram, trying to use him as a shield to ward off more bullets from Valentine. The men danced and pranced in circles, shooting and dodging. Then Valentine saw his chance and dashed straight up to the lawman and blasted him in the face.

The two desperadoes then took off up a side street, firing as they ran. The marshal, seriously wounded and covered with blood, returned the fire while onlookers darted for cover. Two women were slightly injured by stray bullets.

Feeling ran high in Davis City against the Mercers. A posse was quickly formed but Hiram and Valentine got away and made their way into Missouri. Mayor Tillie went to Des Moines and talked to Governor Gear, who issued a proclamation offering a $500 reward for the capture of either Mercer.

A month later the long arm of the law caught up with the fleeing killers near their brother's place in Christian County, Missouri. Peace officers surprised the outlaws and in the resulting gun battle killed Hiram with a load of buckshot. Valentine, wounded in the arm, ran into the woods. The posse found him there later, lying on his face with a terrible gaping wound above his left eye. In despair, Valentine had shot himself in the head with his own .38-caliber Smith & Wesson.

Harry Graves Collection

Actual Photo of the Mercer
Brothers in Their Coffins

The bodies of Hiram and Valentine were returned by train to Leon, the county seat of Decatur County, on December 9. The bandits' coffins were leaned upright against the courthouse in the town square and opened to satisfy local curiosity.

They were taken to the Leon cemetery and laid to rest. The boys' father stood with bowed head during the ceremony, then sadly turned away.

He sighed, "Hiram was a good boy. I would have died gladly for him."

13

Who Stole John Foreman's Calves?

One of the longest and most complicated cases in American legal history started one day in 1874, when S. D. Potter asked his friend Bob Johnson of Jones County to buy him some calves. In the next two decades everybody concerned lived to regret Potter's request.

Johnson, being a neighborly fellow, set out to oblige his friend and in looking around the town of Olin met a stranger who introduced himself as John Smith. Smith claimed he had some good calves for sale and took Johnson to a farm to look at them.

Smith showed Johnson three dark-colored calves and said a fourth one was in the pasture. Johnson liked the animals and bought them, paying cash. Later he drove them to a spot where he was to meet Potter who, according to later testimony, had four light-colored calves in his possession at the time. The calves, light and dark, were all put in a single herd and Potter drove them to his Greene County farm. Everybody went home happy.

Then farmer John Foreman discovered that four of his light-colored calves were missing and set out to find them. He had heard that Potter was in town buying calves and rode into Greene County to look at his herd. Sure enough, there were his four calves. Potter explained to Foreman he purchased the stolen animals from Johnson, so they set out to see him.

They found Bob in Mechanicsville and told him of the missing calves. Johnson related how he had purchased them from John Smith and suggested they should walk over to the new lawyer's office and tell him their problem.

Young attorney Charles Wheeler listened to the farmers and, after mulling the matter over awhile, advised Johnson to pay Foreman for the calves and then swear out a warrant against John Smith for his money.

Bob agreed to this, gave Foreman his note for $24 and then took everybody to the tavern for a friendly drink. Afterward Johnson went back to Olin to find John Smith and discovered nobody had ever heard of the stranger or remembered seeing him in town. Though Johnson was to continue his search for twenty years, the mysterious Mr. Smith was never to be found.

Not long after giving Foreman his note, Bob Johnson heard from a friend that the missing calves were light-colored, whereas the calves he had purchased and delivered to Potter were dark. Bob thought he had been cheated and suspected Potter of stealing Foreman's calves. Accordingly, he refused to pay his note on the grounds that he had received nothing in return and had been deceived. A bank now owned the note and sued Johnson for payment. The first in a long series of courtroom hassles began that resulted in a verdict for the bank and cost the defendant over $1,000 instead of the original $24.

Just to add fuel to the fire, a new organization was started in Jones County called the Anti-Horse Thief Association. Foreman and Potter were charter members of this little social group and through it brought pressure that resulted in the indictment of Bob Johnson by a grand jury for larceny of Foreman's calves.

Meanwhile, Johnson's house caught on fire—through spontaneous combustion, officials said. A hangman's noose was found on his doorstep, and his barn burned to the ground one night—also due to spontaneous combustion! Soon the whole neighborhood was alarmed, causing some farmers to carry firearms as they went about their chores.

Friends urged Johnson to take his family and leave Iowa but he refused. Instead he stayed on and fought his legal battle through several trials until a jury finally acquitted him of the larceny charge. Then he went after revenge. He filed suit for malicious prosecution against seven men, including Potter and Foreman, for $10,000, in order to "get my character back."

For the next twenty years the case was to kick around the courts in five different counties, be argued by more than a score of lawyers and involve over one hundred jurors. Four times the Supreme Court of Iowa reviewed the decision reached by a lower court and reversed it. Before the last loose end of the suit was tied up in 1894, the court costs alone mounted to a staggering $75,000.

But, six trials and many years later, Bob Johnson won his lawsuit and received a judgment for $1,000 against six of the seven defendants. Johnson was exonerated completely in the case of the stolen calves. Bob's faithful attorney, Charles Wheeler, who had stood by him for the entire rugged twenty years, breathed a sigh of relief and would accept for his fee only a broken-down horse and $100 in cash.

His name now cleared, the old farmer went to Anamosa to live out his years and was so respected by that town's citizens they twice elected him mayor. When he died, his fortune recouped and his honor untarnished, the Jones County calf case was only a memory.

So all's well that ends well—except for one thing. No one knows yet who stole John Foreman's calves.

14

The Day They Blew Up the Courthouse

W. W. Van Schaick and Howard Reed should never have pooled their talents in the field of crime. They had lived a life of conspicuous failure in their southern Iowa town of Leon and there wasn't much to indicate they would ever do better—together or individually. Reed had gone broke in the hardware business and Van Schaick was on the same path as proprietor of a Leon stove and tin store. The thought of them teaming up would seem to most people to spell disaster. Even the date they picked to make their debut into crime would indicate an omen of foreboding. It was Sunday, April Fool's Day, 1877.

Actually, Howard and Van had an ambitious plan in mind and one that sounded promising. They knew that some $20,000 was locked in the safe that rested in the vault of the county treasurer's office in the Decatur County courthouse in Leon. The idea, as the two men talked it over, was for them to enter the courthouse by an upstairs window, drill a hole in the floor above the treasurer's office and enter the vault. Here they would rip open the door of the safe and make off into the darkness with the $20,000 loot. On paper it all looked good. So the men gathered up their tools, blasting powder and other useful items of their trade and ventured forth into the early morning darkness of April 1 to carry out their mission.

The first part was easy. Van Schaick and Reed pried up a second story window and started drilling in the floor above what they thought was the treasurer's vault. After toiling some time, the last piece of steel finally gave way and the two men joyously dropped down into the vault. Only one thing was wrong. Instead of getting into the treasurer's vault the robbers had miscalculated and entered the recorder's vault which contained many papers but, alas, no money. The treasurer's office was across the hall.

The Day They Blew Up the Courthouse

Tired but undaunted, the bandits broke off the lock of the recorder's vault and came out into the main office, smashed the door down and went across the hall where they bulldozed their way into the treasurer's office.

At last they ran into a bit of luck. The door to the vault was left unlocked! Inside was the heavy, old safe that contained the fortune.

But time was running out on Reed and Van Schaick. Their efforts had taken most of the early morning hours and it was now nearing 5:00 a.m. Dawn would soon be breaking. Before long people would be up and about. The safe had to be opened and opened fast.

History doesn't record which man dreamed up the idea of blasting but it really doesn't matter. All we know is that they put several pounds of powder under the safe, lit a fuse and ran out into the hall with their hands cupped over their ears. This little explosion, they reckoned, would spring open the safe door and they could run in and scoop up the twenty grand. And so they waited in the hall, counting off the seconds.

And blast it did. But not just a little! Instead, a roar like a thousand cannons boomed through the early morning quiet of the streets of Leon. Dishes rattled in cupboards, houses shook on their foundations and all over town people were leaping from their beds and running outside.

"What happened?" they yelled, "a tornado? An earthquake?"

Meanwhile, back at the courthouse, the bewildered Van Schaick and Reed picked themselves up among the rubble and surveyed their work in amazement. Their blast had erupted with such force that the whole two-story west side of the courthouse was blown out into the yard, including both the treasurer's and recorder's vaults. The object of the explosion, the safe, was thrown out too. It was buried under tons of bricks and wood and smoldering debris, its door still intact and as solid and impenetrable as the Rock of Gibraltar. Surveying the scene, the boys decided the jig was up and departed as fast as they could.

By now the square was full of excited, shouting citizens. W. H. Dake, who lived above a store on the southwest corner of the square, was the first man on the scene. Dake had the presence of mind to grab a pail of water and douse a small blaze, thereby probably saving the entire courthouse from destruction.

Dr. C. D. Scott Collection

The Decatur County Courthouse With Its West Wall Blown Out

As the townspeople looked at the blown-out west wall their hearts were full of rage. "Who is responsible?" they cried. The crowd was relieved when officials found the safe and money intact but that did not help the fact that their courthouse, only three years old, was practically ruined. "Who did this?" they cried again.

Before the morning had passed, suspicion settled on two men—W. W. Van Schaick and Howard Reed. Both had been seen late the night before and, strangely enough, both were missing from their homes.

Sheriff Backus found out that Van had hired a livery team and started for Osceola just after the explosion. Accompanying him was an eighteen-year-old girl he had imported into town a few days earlier. This young lady was described, in the quaint phrasing of the day, as a "fast young bird" and as a "charmer."

The Day They Blew Up the Courthouse

The sheriff immediately sent a telegram to Osceola, some twenty miles north, asking that the couple be apprehended upon their arrival and then he and Deputy Lindsey started off on horseback. Communications being what they were then, the lawmen arrived in Osceola before the telegram and found Van and his charmer and arrested them.

Later that same night officers found Reed sleeping like a baby above Van's store, right across the street from the scene of their ill-fated crime. The lawmen waited till most people were home in bed before taking Reed over to the jail because feeling was so high against the culprits that a lynching was feared.

Van Schaick and Reed, the "April Fools," as they became known, were sentenced to six years in prison at Fort Madison, thus giving them plenty of time to ponder on where they went wrong. The good citizens of Decatur County patched up their courthouse the best they could and it stood for twenty-two years, straight and proud, with hardly a scar showing to remind passersby of its exciting morning on April Fool's Day, 1877.

15

Villisca's Darkest Night

THE hands on the big clock in Ross Moore's drugstore in Villisca stood at 8:30 a.m. as the shrill jangle of the telephone echoed through the store.

The date was Monday, June 10, 1912, and the caller was Mary Peckman, a neighbor of Joe Moore, Ross Moore's brother. Mrs. Peckman told the druggist that something appeared to be wrong at his brother's house as no one was up and about. This was unusual because Joe ran an implement business and went to work before 7:00 a.m. Moore told Mrs. Peckman he would be right out to investigate.

Soon Villisca was stunned by Moore's discovery. Joe Moore, his wife, their four children and two young friends of the family, Lena and Ina Stillinger, had all been slain in the dead of night with an axe! The grisly weapon was found later in the house.

Villisca was in bedlam. Crowds lined the streets and the lawn of the home. People poured into town and every train carried scores of officials, detectives and assorted crackpots. The National Guard was called out to keep order and patrol the streets at night. The local night watchman announced his resignation. Fear spread through the countryside.

The local and county officials, who had never handled a major crime before, proceeded with the investigation. Many blunders were committed by well-intentioned people. The crowds had destroyed footprints in the yard and several had gone through the house. A fingerprint expert was called in from Kansas but said he could not find any prints that were clear. However, it was later testified the "expert" was so intoxicated when he examined the house he could hardly stand up!

As the days drifted into weeks and then months, Villisca slowly returned to normal. Would-be detectives and reporters, discouraged by the lack of clues, quietly left town.

VILLISCA'S DARKEST NIGHT 51

This house, still standing in Villisca, was the scene of the 1912 axe murders. For many years it was vacant, but it is now occupied.

But in 1916, four years after the murders, a persistent Kansas City private detective made an announcement that shocked Villisca almost as much as the crime itself.

Detective J. N. Wilkerson accused a local man, F. F. Jones, of planning the murders. Wilkerson claimed Jones hired a Kansas City thug to kill Joe Moore but the killer went berserk and murdered the entire family. The motive was "business reasons," Wilkerson said.

The accused man was a pillar of the community. He was president of the bank, state senator and former representative in the Iowa legislature. Senator Jones was a wealthy man and owned a considerable amount of real estate in Villisca.

The grand jury refused to indict the senator because of insufficient evidence. Later Jones sued Wilkerson and several Villisca residents for slander but was not awarded damages.

Wilkerson held mass meetings to raise money for his campaign to indict Jones and collected thousands of dollars. When he left Villisca a few years later the detective was much better off financially for his stay. Senator Jones, in his sixties, saw an end to his political career. Those familiar with the case today feel Jones was another innocent victim of the horrible murders.

A year after the Jones episode, word of an eccentric Sutton, Nebraska, Presbyterian minister reached Villisca authorities. The minister, Reverend Lyn G. J. Kelly, was upsetting local residents by darting behind trees late at night and yelling, "They're after me. They think I killed them at Villisca."

Investigation revealed Reverend Kelly, who was soon dubbed "The Little Minister" because he was only five feet tall and weighed around one hundred ten pounds, had been in Villisca the night of the murders and preached at the church Sunday night where the Moore family and Stillinger girls had attended. He was brought back to Red Oak, the county seat, and indicted by the grand jury for the axe murders.

Later, Kelly confessed. He said that he stayed in Villisca that night and went for a late walk. Chancing by the Moore home, he noticed an axe leaning against the woodpile. Then he said he received a command "from God" to go and ". . . slay, slay utterly."

The opening day of the Kelly trial the "Little Minister" repudiated his confession, saying it was made under duress. The grand jury also criticized the Iowa attorney general for methods used in obtaining the confession.

The main case left against Kelly was the testimony of S. Barnett. Barnett said he lived in Macedonia and saw Kelly shortly after the preacher arrived in town from Villisca the morning the murders were discovered. Kelly also lived in Macedonia in 1912. Barnett said the preacher told him of the crime around 8:00 a.m. which was before Villisca even knew of the murders.

However, other witnesses disputed Barnett's claim, saying it was the Monday two weeks following the crime that Kelly told of the murders.

On September 28, 1917, the Kelly jury was dismissed because of its failure to arrive at a verdict. The poll had been eleven for acquittal and one for conviction. When the announcement was made, Wilkerson, Ross Moore and other members of the victims' families rushed up to congratulate Kelly. The "Little Minister" was freed.

Kelly soon disappeared from sight and despite the efforts of the Iowa Bureau of Investigation and several interested persons, his whereabouts, dead or alive, are not known today. To add to the mystery the complete records of the trial are missing from the Red Oak courthouse and no one knows what happened to them.

After a half-century the Villisca axe murders remain unsolved. The town today is divided in opinion as to who committed the savage crime. The house still stands in Villisca and the axe weapon was given to this writer by Mrs. James Risdon, widow of the former head of the Iowa Bureau of Criminal Investigation.

Although most of the principals in the case are gone, the crime will never be completely forgotten. On the edge of town in a quiet little cemetery, eight tombstones still serve as silent reminders of the terrible tragedy and the many, many questions that even the passing of more than half a century have failed to answer.

16

Buried Gold and Watchful Ghosts

TAKE a murder, add a dash of buried treasure, mix in a story of a vengeful ghost and a suspicious lawyer; then implicate four well-known old gentlemen in a peaceful country town and you should come up with the recipe for a whale of a good story.

And that's exactly what happened years ago in the village of Siam, nestled in the hills of Taylor County in southwestern Iowa.

The whole tale started to unfold in 1914 when seventy-two-year-old Sam Anderson walked into the Chariton law office of W. W. Bulman and told the attorney he wanted to start suit against four Taylor County men.

Anderson, who had just moved from Siam, told Bulman of how he had settled on his father-in-law's farm near Siam thirty-five years earlier and started farming. One day he was visited by the Huntsman brothers who had an adjoining farm. Bates Huntsman told Anderson that three separate trunks of treasure containing $90,000, $50,000 and $12,000 were buried somewhere in the area of the Huntsman and Anderson farms.

The Huntsman boys told Sam he could have one-fourth of the treasure if he would agree to dig anytime requested. To this Anderson readily consented. Thus began a fantastic, twenty-five year search for hidden riches. Anderson never knew when he might be called away from his farming chores to dig for gold. Many times the trio worked late at night. On one such night, according to Anderson, a screaming ghost appeared and chased them from a locust grove they were searching.

Anderson's complaint was that one night he uncovered a tin box but Bates Huntsman pulled a gun on him and took it away. Anderson claimed part of the treasure was in the box and he was never given his promised share.

When the old farmer finished his story Attorney Bulman was suspicious. Where had the money come from in the first place? Anderson claimed

BURIED GOLD AND WATCHFUL GHOSTS 55

he didn't know but Huntsman had said it was from a cattle sale years earlier. There was enough sincerity in Anderson's talk that the lawyer agreed to investigate his case. For the next year Bulman tracked down leads, became fascinated with the stranger-than-fiction tale and put together the theory that was to shock Iowa.

In 1915 Bulman dropped his bombshell right into the lap of peaceful Taylor County. He filed information charging four respected Taylor County men, Nathaniel Damewood, sixty-one, his brother, John, sixty-four, Sam Scrivner, seventy-four, and Bates Huntsman, seventy-seven, with the murder in 1868 of a wealthy cattleman and a young boy near Siam. Bulman said a trunk of money, some of it in gold, worth over $100,000 was stolen and buried in Taylor County.

According to Bulman, the four accused and two other men now deceased had a gang that carried out the killing of a Missouri cattle buyer and a young boy companion, dumped the man's body in a well near Siam and buried the lad in a locust grove. The loot was then hidden on the Huntsman or Anderson farm in three different spots and a map was made showing the location of each. However, the map was burned in a fire that destroyed the Huntsman cabin. Since none of the men could remember where the treasure was they commenced the search that was to last a quarter of a century.

Taylor County and all Iowa was aghast at the lawyer's charge. Even the Iowa attorney general, greatly agitated because he knew nothing about the case until Bulman filed charges, went to Bedford, the county seat, to attend the hearing.

When the big day arrived the streets of Bedford were packed with buggies as the whole countryside came to enjoy the show. The July heat was sweltering in the little courtroom as eight hundred people crowded through its doors.

The four defendants, looking "haggard and drawn," pleaded not guilty as the exuberant Bulman presented his case. The lawyer told the spectators his version of the crime and also implicated a local physician, the late Dr. Golliday, in the murders. Many townspeople recalled how "Doc" Golliday had been found dead in his vine-tangled shack a few years back with thousands of dollars scattered about. People had wondered then where old Doc had gotten his money but most thought he had saved it as his last years were spent as a recluse.

Then Bulman dramatically presented a "mystery witness," Maria Collins Porter. Mrs. Porter, a ". . . little, old brown-faced lady with a bonnet," took the stand and testified that as a girl of fourteen she had seen the defendants carry the body of a man through the woods. She said the gang saw her and threatened to kill her if she ever talked.

Mrs. Porter said one of the members of the gang, appropriately named Jonathan Dark, was married to her sister and often said he would kill her. A few years later Dark told Mrs. Porter her time was up and started for her. Mrs. Porter's sister happened in just then and shot Dark dead. The little lady added from the witness chair, "I held his head with one hand and a bucket to catch the blood with my other." A shudder could almost be heard throughout the courtroom.

However, any real evidence was lacking. There was no body, no weapon, no treasure. Just the story of an old lady and a weary farmer, put together by a brash lawyer. After the hearing of Bulman's "evidence," Justice of the Peace Sawyer granted a defense motion to dismiss the case. The four men charged with murder went home free men, much to the joy of most of Taylor County.

Was there a murder? Are thousands of dollars still buried somewhere in Taylor County? Are two bodies sleeping near Siam in unmarked graves?

Nobody knows. That is, perhaps nobody but the ghost the oldtimers say still flits around the locust grove on the old Huntsman farm.

17

Hey! That's John Dillinger!

There have been many exciting events in Iowa's past but few can compare in action and drama with the day John Dillinger invaded Mason City.

Dillinger and his men blazed into town, terrorized citizens, looted the bank and roared off some $50,000 richer. It was a big day for Public Enemy No. 1 and a day that Mason City will probably never forget. But it was also a day in a chain of events that presents vivid proof that crime doesn't pay—for very long.

John Dillinger was a thirty-one-year-old outlaw with an embittered disposition and a surly, lop-sided sneer. He had already spent nine years of his life in Indiana prisons.

Dillinger had gathered around him a gang of other toughs including a brazen, trigger-happy punk named Baby Face Nelson who was notorious in his own right. The bandits started out in June of 1933 with a bank holdup, a supermarket robbery and a drugstore stickup in one day. Then they roamed the Midwest, cleaning out banks and leaving a path of violence. They decided Mason City would be their next target and drove into town on March 13, 1934.

The big Buick sedan quietly double parked at the rear of the First National Bank at 2:40 p.m. The six men took their positions like clockwork. Two went inside, a third stood in the front doorway and another remained with the car. One man stationed himself in front of Mulcahy's drugstore across the street from the bank. Dillinger paced nervously up and down in front of the bank with a machine gun.

Before anyone really knew what was happening the bandits slipped into the bank and had it under control.

"Hands up!" one of the thieves roared at H. C. Fisher, assistant cashier. He ordered Fisher to open the vault or "we'll bore you full of holes." Fisher complied and the robber scooped up bundles of five-dollar bills. While this was going on the other men were cleaning out the desk tills.

The bank guard, Tom Walters, was perched in his bulletproof cage overlooking the lobby and tried to fire at the invaders. But Dillinger's men acted so quickly that each man used one of the local residents as a shield.

The first man grabbed was F. A. Stephenson who was at a teller's window writing a check. The thief used Stephenson to prevent the guard from returning fire while he trained his machine gun on Walter's cage. All the guard could do was fire a few tear gas pellets that soon fogged the bank.

Meanwhile the shots caused a large crowd to gather outside, although the snarling Dillinger kept any help at bay. He interspersed his outbursts of laughter with random shots from his machine gun. Suddenly a young man in a new Hudson came innocently driving down the street. "Get back," Dillinger screamed and filled the radiator full of lead as spectators scrambled. Dillinger also exchanged shots with Officer James Buchanan who ducked behind a G. A. R. monument across the street. The boulder was chipped by the gunfire.

Baby Face Nelson added his contribution to the afternoon by his unprovoked firing on the crowd, hitting R. L. James, secretary of the Mason City school board, in the leg. Another series of shots by Dillinger peppered the windows of the I. O. O. F. Building.

The tear gas caused the men to make their escape leaving thousands of dollars behind. They herded over a dozen customers and bank employees outside, made some stand on the running boards and drove out of town. They ordered the hostages to keep their eyes focused straight ahead and not to move.

Clarence McGowan of Mason City was slightly injured by shots as he attempted to follow the car. The gunmen dropped roofing tacks along the way to discourage pursuit but the hostages were released unharmed a few miles east of town. The Buick, which had been stolen, was later found abandoned and the gang with their loot of $52,000 had disappeared.

For days afterward the big bank robbery was the talk of Mason City. Crowds lined up to see the bullet holes in the bank and listened avidly

Hey! That's John Dillinger! 59

while those who had been in the bank at the time told of the excitement. The *Globe-Gazette* printed many accounts of the robbery by those who had been taken captive during the getaway.

Dillinger's mob went on to other bank jobs but their luck started to run thin. Only three weeks after the Mason City job, Eddie Green, who had been stationed inside the bank, was killed in St. Paul by an F. B. I. agent. Another mobster was shot and killed less than one month later. Tommy Carroll, driver of the getaway car, was killed in Waterloo during a battle with city police.

In July, Dillinger, who had just been named Public Enemy No. 1 by the F. B. I., was betrayed in Chicago by the "woman in red" and breathed his last in a dirty alley. He was killed by Agent Melvin Purvis as he attempted to draw his gun.

Homer Van Meter, who had been in the Mason City drugstore doorway, was shot down in St. Paul a few weeks later.

The last member of the gang, the terrible Baby Face Nelson, was wounded on November 27, 1934, by two agents who also were killed in a raging gun battle near Chicago. Nelson escaped but his nineteen bullet wounds were too much and the next day his body was found stripped of clothing in a ditch twenty miles away.

By Thanksgiving Day, 1934, only nine months after their day of glory in Mason City, all six members of the John Dillinger Gang were in their graves.

PART THREE

Favorite Stories of Hawkeyeland

18

Spirit Lake and the City Slicker

THE oldtimers in Spirit Lake like to tell of the time long ago when their fathers put a city slicker in his place, frightened him out of town and ended up with one of the best jokes ever played in Iowa.

The target for Spirit Lake's humorous arrow was found in the person of Charles Swift of Philadelphia, Pennsylvania. Mr. Swift was a drummer who arrived in town one day in 1885.

This was the first time Swift had ever ventured west of the Mississippi and he didn't find life on the frontier too pleasant. For one thing, cinders from the train had charred his elegant clothes and there was absolutely no culture in Iowa. The people were even worse. They were barbarian, ill-mannered, dirty—absolutely terrible!

Now if Mr. Swift had thought these things but not expressed them, the local residents might not have had reason to be unhappy. But the drummer was not that type of person. Instead, he daily made the rounds of the few business places and repeated to anyone willing to listen his views of the West. Since Swift's stay in town was to be an extended visit, his pronouncements soon became rather tiresome. In fact, many folks began to think this dude was actually insulting them.

One day Swift was telling the local liveryman, Dick Speed, how dreary life was in the West and that the eastern image of cowboys and Indians was romantic nonsense. "Why," he said, "I haven't even seen a cowboy in Iowa."

This last statement put the wheels of Speed's mind speeding. When the obnoxious Easterner left, the liveryman made the rounds of all the stores calling the businessmen to a meeting that evening in his stable.

The next afternoon Mr. Swift was sitting in the lobby of Spirit Lake's only hotel complaining to an old, deaf gentleman of the ways of the West. Suddenly the lobby doors flew open and a tall, rough looking hombre

SPIRIT LAKE AND THE CITY SLICKER 63

loomed over the threshold. He was dressed in heavy chaps, black vest, big sombrero and sported two six-shooters at his side.

While Swift and the old man looked on in surprise, the cowboy stalked over to the hotel desk and started yelling at the clerk, a little fellow named Harry. Louder and louder the argument got until the cowboy pulled one of his guns and shot straight at poor Harry.

The clerk yelped in pain, clasped his chest and dramatically fell over the counter. Since his hand had been full of a red substance, his shirt immediately was covered with what looked like a gusher of blood. This, along with Harry's groaning and writhing on the floor, presented a spectacle to behold.

The old fellow, who was practically the only person in town besides Swift that wasn't in on the gag, jumped from his chair, threw his cane to the winds and ran down the street yelling "murder!"

Swift, too stunned to move, watched in horror as one of the hotel maids came down the stairs, looked things over nonchalantly, and then dragged Harry out by his feet.

When Swift's senses returned he dashed outside and ran to a group of men standing on the street. "Help," he cried, "there's been a killing. Harry's been murdered!"

"Harry, eh?" one of the frontiersmen drawled. "Not much of a loss. Fellow's consumptive, been livin' over a year now jest to save funeral expenses."

"Suppose Bear Fight's on a spree again," chimed in another. "Bodies'll be piled high 'fore long. He always does a neat job of drillin'."

The men told Swift that when Bear Fight got around to him they would send his body back to Pennsylvania to his widow if he would leave some money for the fare.

By this time the "city fella" was so shaken that he sneaked through alleys back to his hotel lest Bear Fight see him. Just as he safely made it to his room and shut and bolted the door, shots rang out from the street below. Peeking out his window, Swift saw men pouring out of a saloon across the street. "Bear Fight's shootin' up the town agin," they yelled. The salesman hid under his bed the rest of the day and night.

The next day, after checking around corners to see that Bear Fight wasn't around, the Easterner went to county officials and offered to testify in court about the shooting. The official, who was also in on the gag, told Swift that the last man who had testified had been shot fifty times and burned to a crisp right in his cell.

At this news, Swift changed his mind about testifying, but the official threatened to hold him in jail as a material witness or make him pay $5,000 bail. The salesman, scared out of his wits by now, said he would go and raise the money but actually stole away and took the first train out of town.

The jokers then telegraphed the train about the "escape" and the conductor began to question the passengers. When Swift saw this he slipped out of the coach into the baggage car where he bribed the baggageman to hide him between mail sacks until out of the state.

In that way, riding with mail sacks as a cover and the baggage car floor as a bed, the city slicker from the East escaped forever from Wild Western Iowa.

19

The Vision in the Wildwood

> Oh, come, come, come, come,
> Come to the church in the wildwood
> Oh, come to the church in the vale;
> No spot is so dear to my childhood
> As the little brown church in the vale.

ON SUNDAY mornings the world over this refrain drifts from the windows of the churches of the land; from the little frame buildings in the country to the huge brick structures of the cities.

Religious people everywhere join to sing the lilting strains of "The Little Brown Church in the Vale." One of the most popular hymns ever written, it is difficult to find a hymnal that does not include this song.

"The Little Brown Church in the Vale" has been translated into several different languages and has enjoyed universal acceptance.

Yet, few people know the strange story behind the writing of this song.

The tale started on a warm summer forenoon in 1857. A young man, William S. Pitts, was riding by stage into the valley of the Little Cedar River in northeastern Iowa. Pitts was from Wisconsin and was riding into Iowa to visit his future wife at Fredericksburg.

The dusty stage stopped for the noon hour and to change horses at the busy town of Bradford, which no longer exists but was then located two miles northeast of the present town of Nashua.

After taking his dinner, the young Pitts took a walk down Cedar Street. As he leisurely strolled along that beautiful summer day he came upon a lovely spot of oaks and cedars which, as he said later, "seemed to stand as though waiting expectant, calling—." As he gazed at the scene the vision of a song danced through his head.

Returning to board the stage, William Pitts kept the vision in the wildwood in his heart and when back home in Wisconsin he wrote the song.

In Pitts' own words: *As I pondered on this Iowa experience, I came to realize that what was needed to complete the picture was a little church, a little brown church in the wildwood—a church and a bell calling, come, come, come. Gradually words and music came to give form to my vision. They were written down and laid aside and I found that only then was I at peace with myself.*

The song was laid aside and, for a while, forgotten.

But the story is not yet finished. Pitts was married the following year and in 1862 he and his wife returned to her home in Fredericksburg. Pitts, a school teacher who later became a physician, was called the next fall to teach singing in Bradford.

As the young school teacher rode horseback to take up his new assignment he decided to ride by the site that had given rise to his vision and song six years earlier.

When he rode down Cedar Street to the beautiful spot in the wildwood, Pitts was amazed to find a church—a brown church with a bell—standing among the dark cedars and oaks. The scene was just like his vision of six years ago!

The Vision in the Wildwood

The church had been built just recently by volunteers under the direction of the Congregational minister, Reverend John Nutting. They had painted the church brown because it was the cheapest paint available.

So the beautiful song now known the world over was written from a vision which, before the song was ever sung or printed, came to life. Later, Pitts brought his singing students to the church and for the first time in public the song, "The Little Brown Church in the Vale," was sung in the new little building that is now a famous shrine.

Now, more than one hundred years after the writing of the song, the Little Brown Church near Nashua attracts over one hundred thousand persons every year. Around one thousand couples are united in marriage yearly at its altar. The Little Brown Church has indeed become one of the most famous churches in the world.

Thanks to a curious twist of fate, William Pitts' vision and William Pitts' song will live forever.

20

The Town That Fetes the Hobos

EVERY year in August the Weary Willies, hobos, tramps and beggars of America beat a path to a little town in north central Iowa.

For sixty-two years Britt, in Hancock County, has been known as Hobo Haven. The Knights of the Road return annually to hold their national convention, elect their officers and enjoy two days of food and frolic.

And of all the conventions, none can match the very first. It took the whole town by surprise, caused reporters from all over the nation to swarm into Britt's streets, and ended up embarrassing one of America's most prominent men.

The idea for Britt's hobo convention grew out of an item that appeared in a Chicago newspaper in 1900. The account told of how a number of hobos had gathered at Danville, Illinois, for a meeting.

T. A. Potter, a Britt businessman, read the article and his curiosity became aroused. He wrote to the secretary of the organization requesting more information.

Some time later Potter received a reply which he showed to the local editor, E. N. Bailey. Together, they conceived the idea of a hobo convention in their own town.

Potter and Bailey made a proposal to the hobos' representative, Big Brother Charles F. Noe, for his group to hold a meeting in Britt. In return the town would supply a carload of beer and feed every man for two days.

Mr. Noe, along with "Onion" Cotton, "Head Pipe" of the organization, paid a visit to Britt and found it satisfactory for their particular needs. The offer was accepted and August 22, 1900, was set for the National Hobo Convention. It has been claimed that this was the first national

By Don Grodt

On the Road to Britt

convention of any type ever held in Iowa—a claim not widely advertised by the state.

Most townspeople regarded the whole thing as a joke and did not expect many hobos or spectators to show up. However, events soon changed their minds.

The day before the gathering, crowds started to arrive. Thanks to a great deal of newspaper publicity, word had spread throughout the nation about the unusual event. From far and near people flocked to Britt. Interest was so great that reporters from sixteen large daily papers were present.

And tramps—from all over they poured in. Every train passing through dumped its cargo of hobo humanity into Britt's waiting arms. Before long, over two hundred fifty assorted "bo's" were milling around enjoying the free food and drink.

The town was decorated for the big occasion with banners, tin cans and other suitable articles. The "guests" were taken to the fair grounds and given quarters in the barns.

For entertainment, ball games, foot races and horse races were provided. For the less athletic, there were long games of cards and checkers. Many were just content to rest and drink.

One of the main features of the event was the drawing up of a political platform and the nominating of a candidate for the 1900 presidential election. The hobos went on record as opposing President McKinley because he "believed in giving work to every man."

The platform committee, meeting in the shade of a water tank, came up with the following suggestions:

1. All bulldogs shall be muzzled.
2. No baths shall be allowed for anyone.
3. Free and unlimited distribution of beer.
4. No housewife shall offer any hobo mince pie of her own making.

After accepting the platform, the convention set about the task of choosing their presidential candidate. One "Nebuchadnezzar Lloyd" of Utah nominated Admiral Dewey, saying, ". . . he is one of us, because he never had but one home and he gave that away. He believes in free trade, imperialism, silver, gold, and everything else that is repudiated by the other parties." Lloyd's stirring speech was successful; Admiral Dewey was nominated unanimously.

Papers around the nation noted Dewey's nomination in Iowa by a group of hobos. One paper ran a cartoon showing the nominating committee of shabby tramps traveling to Washington in a box car. It was said Dewey was quite embarrassed by the confidence the country's hobos had expressed in him.

When the gala affair was over the drifters hit the road and rails and departed. Only five or six remained in Britt the day after the convention closed.

The townspeople returned to their everyday life and suddenly realized they had enjoyed the show and all the publicity. They offered to host the convention again the following year and now, over a half-century later, Britt is known throughout the country as the town that fetes the hobos.

21

When the Sun Hid Her Head

In Iowa history, 1869 is remembered as the year when the chickens went to roost early.

August 7, 1869, was the date for a heavenly show—the total eclipse of the sun. The eclipse of 1963 was similar to the time in our state's past when the attention of the whole nation was focused on the wondrous celestial display.

Iowa was in an ideal position to view the result of the moon coming in a direct line between the sun and the earth. For this reason many of America's most noted astronomers came to Iowa and set up shop.

The Franklin Institute of Philadelphia and the United States Navy sent men to Burlington, Mount Pleasant, Ottumwa and Oskaloosa. The Naval Observatory in Washington also established stations in Des Moines and Cedar Falls. An English and a Canadian astronomer journeyed to Jefferson to study the big event. The purpose of working in so many areas was to avoid bad local weather conditions.

Not all of the scientists were men, however. One writer reported:

Miss Maria Mitchell, a noted astronomer of Vassar College, brought to Burlington a class of eight girls interested in the eclipse. Dressed in the height of fashion, with their wide hoop skirts and tiny parasols, and schooled in ladylike demeanor, they lent a touch of romance to the occasion.

Elaborate preparations were made at Burlington to photograph the eclipse. A photographic team consisted of four or five men who worked together like clockwork to obtain a series of good negatives.

One of the men prepared the plates—each had to be coated with a special gelatin preparation and then impregnated with silver nitrate; one man operated the camera, another timed the exposure and the last developed the negatives in the nearby dark room immediately after exposure. The job was tricky, but the men were so skilled that forty-one negatives out of forty-two were good.

While the scientists prepared for the eclipse the event became the talk of the countryside. For weeks in advance it was discussed on town squares, in newspapers and around firesides.

Many Iowans didn't understand the details of the phenomenon but they were interested because they had heard this was the first time a white man in our state had ever viewed such an occurrence.

There were those, however, who did not like the astronomers' presence. Some said they were prying "into God's secrets." A man in Mount Pleasant went about town days beforehand declaring that God had "veiled His sun in order to baffle them." Another prophet pronounced the eclipse ". . . a judgment upon the world for its abomination," and the path of its shadow over the earth would "be marked by utter blight."

August 7 dawned warm and clear as Iowans watched the sky for the first sign of darkness. When it came, the sky changed from blue to a livid purple. Objects became yellowish and the figures of people cast an "unearthly cadaverous aspect." Temperatures dropped throughout the state and a light dew was precipitated at Cedar Falls.

When the Sun Hid Her Head

Cattle became uneasy and went along bellowing as they made their way toward the stable. Birds flocked together and old hens ran about, clucking frantically as they gathered their broods under their wings. Chickens, turkeys and other barnyard fowl sought their roosts, "wondering no doubt who moved up the clock and compelled them to go to bed on half-empty gizzards."

As Iowans craned their necks and the scientists manned their instruments, total darkness prevailed.

The complete eclipse was reported to be "somewhat less intense than that which prevails at night in the presence of a full moon." As the darkness settled, the chime of the crickets and the cry of the whip-poor-will came from the woods. Work in the fields and in the homes stopped and the whole world seemed to quiet down. Rugged pioneers stood in awe of nature's wonders. Near Mount Pleasant a small group of white-robed fanatics sat on a hillside and silently awaited what they were sure would be the end of the world.

The darkness lasted about three minutes and then it was all over. The fowl and the cattle were bewildered by the short night, children ventured back outside alone, men started back to work in the fields and the scientists packed their gear and left the Hawkeye state.

But for a long time afterwards people talked of the day of darkness. Family events were dated as happening before or after the eclipse. Old diaries were full of accounts of the exciting event. The eclipse had come and gone but Iowans would always remember the day in 1869 when the sun hid her head.

22

Jumbo on a Rampage

For one year and two months the "Eighth Wonder of the World" gushed through the streets of Belle Plaine, leaving in its wake tons of sand, thousands of rocks, many jangled nerves—and a mighty good story.

The whole thing started in 1886 when William Weir was hired to dig a well for the city of Belle Plaine. Little did the town know it was standing on the threshold of fame.

Weir was to receive the princely sum of $350 for his labors to provide water for the south part of town and the schoolhouse. He started his work with a two-inch drill on a fine August day, hoping to complete the job in less than a week. But fate shook her head and smiled.

After digging one hundred ninety-three feet and striking water, Weir left the job for the day. That evening, strollers noticed a little stream of water belching from the uncapped hole.

Bright and early the next morning, Weir returned to the scene and was surprised by the amount of water spurting in the air. As the day wore on the flow increased. By late afternoon it was a monster, shooting eight feet high and a foot and one-half in circumference. Mr. Weir decided he was not a well man and quickly left town.

By late evening the gusher was the talk of the town and many people were frightened. What if the fountain got bigger and washed the whole town away?

The city council was spurred into action by such talk and called an emergency meeting. But what could be done with an artesian well that wouldn't stop? Finally they decided to get a pile driver and force piling down the well's mouth. Several days were spent locating such a machine, but it was discovered this wouldn't work anyhow.

By this time the rampaging fountain was shooting up over five million gallons each twenty-four hours. The once two-inch hole was now

JUMBO ON A RAMPAGE

expanded to three feet in diameter as rocks, sand, wood, bones and pebbles roared from its mouth.

Townspeople nicknamed the artesian well "Jumbo" and proudly hailed it as the "Eighth Wonder of the World." People poured in for miles around to see the wondrous fountain.

Newspapers picked up the story and, as seemed to have been the custom in those days, didn't let the truth get in the way of a good tale. Reports were grossly exaggerated.

One paper described the gusher as, "Water spouting hundreds of feet in the air with a roar that could be heard for miles." Another, an illustrated paper, wrote in lurid detail of the well and included a drawing showing people being rescued by boats from upper stories of houses! An imaginative reporter even blamed Jumbo for somehow causing the Charleston earthquake which occurred a few days later.

Even though things weren't nearly as bad as the papers said, they were bad enough. Jumbo was a nuisance that had outgrown its novelty. Months dragged by and still the water poured. Two streams over twelve feet wide and one foot deep were necessary to carry the water to the Iowa River. Tons of sand were left in city streets and on lawns.

Even though chemists reported the water was unfit to drink, many did drink it and claimed it had great medicinal qualities. One man said his doctor had given him only four weeks to live but after drinking the water his troubles disappeared and his health improved.

Many other attempts were made to close the pesky well but they were all unsuccessful. The council became increasingly worried and signed a contract with a Marshalltown man named King to cap the well for $2,000.

King arrived in Belle Plaine and first started building a high board fence around Jumbo. When asked why, King said he planned to charge twenty-five cents admission to watch him work. The council put a stop to this and reminded King he was hired to cap the well, not make a show of it. He worked until May of 1887 and succeeded only in cutting down the flow slightly. King offered to settle with the council for $1,800 but was refused. The disgusted contractor then walked off the job muttering threats about suing the city.

As a last resort the council hired a local foundry to work on the persistent well. The hometown boys devised a complicated system of hydraulic jacks and, with the help of great quantities of sand and cement, Jumbo was finally closed on October 6, 1887.

Before filling the beast, its hungry mouth had swallowed over two hundred feet of pipe, forty carloads of stone, and one hundred thirty barrels of cement. Just to play it safe, an asphalt road was laid over Jumbo's last resting place and the whole town sighed with relief.

But even so, they say that for many years people walked around the spot and kept a watchful eye on its grave. They were always just a little bit afraid that someday old Jumbo would shoot right up through all that concrete and asphalt and once again show the people of Belle Plaine who was boss.

23

A Palace of Corn

In the late 1880's a rash of strange buildings sprouted up in different sections of Iowa that caused quite a bit of comment throughout the nation. These were large "palaces" covered with whatever was an outstanding product of the area in which it was built. Creston had its Blue Grass Palace, Ottumwa its Coal Palace, Algona a Hay Palace and Davenport even talked of an Onion Palace! But the first one, the one that started the palace craze, was the most original and fantastic of them all—Sioux City's Palace of Corn.

The idea for a structure to symbolize a leading crop occurred to a group of prominent Sioux City businessmen one day in August, 1887. Sioux City was a rapidly growing and prosperous town with a great future ahead. Why not build a structure of corn to show publicly an expression of thanks for the great crops and the city's tremendous growth?

The idea met with enthusiastic approval and plans were formulated for the building. At first it was estimated that $5,000 would do the job but this was later raised to $25,000. By late September the project had taken on so much importance that the Sioux City Corn Palace Exposition Company was organized and incorporated with a capital stock of $250,000.

The morning of October 3, 1887, dawned on a city of corn. Illuminated arches spanned the intersections of the streets, stores and houses were decked out with flags and bunting, and everywhere there was corn, corn, corn. A gala atmosphere prevailed over the town and there was plenty to do, see and hear. But the big attraction was the pride and joy of Sioux City—their Corn Palace.

The two-hundred-square-foot building looked like it might have been taken out of Alice in Wonderland. At the front were square towers representing Dakota, Nebraska and Minnesota. Great arched entrances opened through smaller towers to the streets. Above each doorway was a panel depicting an agricultural scene.

The towers were connected by walls and in the center of the structure was a green, corn-thatched roof. A cupola towered over the center of the roof with a spire rising to a height of one hundred feet. A flag designating the name of a neighboring state waved from the corner tower and a Sioux City banner proudly pinnacled the spire. The many towers and arches "... contributed an appearance of airiness and whimsicality quite in keeping with the ornate exterior." The entire outer surface of the building was covered with corn and other grains.

Inside the palace was a large auditorium chock-full with exhibits of the work of Mother Nature. Brilliant colors of grain, grass and straw adorned the walls. A map of the United States was on display that was made from seeds, each state in a different color. A huge carrot spider was poised in a web of corn fibers and, most striking of all, was a beautiful wax figure clad in a robe of satin husks and bearing a cornstalk scepter, standing upon a stairway of yellow corn.

The highlight of the week-long celebration was the arrival of President Grover Cleveland and his wife. Cleveland was on a tour of the country and was greatly impressed by the Corn Palace. He remarked that this was the first new thing he had seen on his trip.

Two eastern millionaires, Chauncey Depew and Cornelius Vanderbilt, also came to view the wonder. Mr. Depew said, "Any city so enterprising and so prolific in beautiful designs, and enthusiastic in all public enterprises must of necessity be the metropolis of the northwest."

When the festival was over the event was deemed such a success that immediate plans were made for a similar celebration the following year. Five more were held, each with a different corn palace.

The fifth and last palace was really the most magnificent and beautiful of them all. Opened on October 1, 1891, the structure was more than a block long and dominated by a majestic dome two hundred feet high. This palace was so well designed and so graceful that it was acclaimed an architectural masterpiece.

The front of the palace was an immense arch over the street with a large balcony at each end. The arch was covered with red corn. The great center dome was covered with oats and its base was decorated with

A Palace of Corn

Sioux City's Fifth and Last Corn Palace in 1891

animals of dark seeds and grasses against a blue background. White, purple, red, orange and yellow indigo corn added to the dazzling color scheme of the turret-adorned structure.

"To be thoroughly appreciated," wrote a visitor, "the Palace should be seen at sunset, when the solid mass of the building is cast in shade. Then each tower and turret and minaret shines in the warm light as if wrought of gold, like some magnificent dream of Spanish castles discerned above the mist which fancy dares not penetrate."

Inside, the walls of the auditorium sported many paintings and statues constructed of grain. A miniature library was the favorite exhibit with its tiny walls bearing pictures and a maid with an apron of flowers. The floor was covered with a grass rug. Upon a table were quill pens of cane and straw, a corn lamp and a gourd inkwell. The main floor was decorated with Spanish moss and brake grass.

Although the fifth festival was very successful and ran for three weeks, it was the last. The corn palace idea seemed to have run its course and its backers decided to quit while they were ahead.

Even so, for years to come old-timers would tell stories to other generations about the wonderful celebrations and, most of all, about Sioux City's magnificent golden palaces of corn.

24

The Cardiff Giant

It's ironic that the idea for the most successful hoax ever pulled on an unsuspecting public was born during a Sunday church service in Ackley, Iowa.

In the summer of 1868, George Hull had reluctantly accompanied friends he was visiting to the Methodist Church in Ackley. Hull was a confidence man at heart and an atheist by nature.

But that Sunday the minister spoke of the resurrection and of biblical giants. For some reason this caught the doubting Hull's fancy and set the wheels of his scheming mind into motion.

A few days later, Hull and a friend journeyed to Fort Dodge where a seven-thousand-pound block of gypsum was purchased and shipped by them to a sculptor's studio in Chicago. The weeks flew by as Hull and the sculptor worked over the gypsum. When the men finished their task the block of stone had emerged a monster.

A giant ten feet tall and three feet in breadth at the shoulders had been carved from the gypsum. The features were of a man with one arm on his body and one leg raised slightly higher than the other, as if contracted in pain. To the excited Hull, his handiwork presented a million possibilities.

From Chicago the colossus was shipped to Cardiff, New York. It was then hauled to the farm of Hull's cousin, William Newell, and buried. There it remained, lifeless and unknown, for over a year.

In October, 1869, Newell hired two men for the ostensible purpose of digging a well. Naturally, instead of hitting water they struck the giant.

Quickly word spread of the amazing discovery at Bill Newell's place. Some called it a petrified man; others said it was an Indian prophet; a few thought it an ancient carving. But whatever people thought it was, they all wanted to see it.

The enterprising Hull and Newell erected a board fence around the scene and put a large tent over the sleeping figure. An admission of fifty cents was charged just to see it.

As more and more people talked of the discovery the crowds increased. The little farm resembled a county fair as people from near and far lined up to take a look at a real giant. It was estimated that the men took in over $1,000 on good days.

Andrew White, president of Cornell University, visited Cardiff and wrote the following account:

The roads were crowded with buggies, carriages, and even omnibuses from the city, and with lumber-wagons from the farms—all laden with passengers. Entering the tent we saw a large pit or grave, and, at the bottom of it, perhaps five feet below the surface, an enormous figure. Lying in its grave, with the subdued light from the roof of the tent falling upon it, and with the limbs contorted as if in a death struggle, it produced a most weird effect. An air of great solemnity pervaded the place. Visitors hardly spoke above a whisper.

Newspaper reporters converged on the farm and sent glowing reports back to their papers, adding to the giant's reputation. Word of the oddity spread throughout the nation and many foreign countries followed news of the strange discovery. Scientists examined the figure and many wrote long and scholarly reports, citing the giant as a relic from another age. One pointed to what he thought was erosion on the body to confirm that it had been buried for centuries.

Even the great showman, P. T. Barnum, wanted to buy the giant but a group of New York men joined together and beat him to it. They gave Hull $40,000 for three-fourths of his interest.

However, there were a few skeptics. A Professor Marsh of Yale examined the figure and pronounced it a "decided humbug." Still, the crowds that lined up to see the giant weren't interested in the opinion of a few scientists. After all, many other scientists had examined it and found it authentic.

One day a smart lawyer from Fort Dodge, Iowa, visited the exhibit and thought the colossus resembled Iowa gypsum. His keen mind sensed something fraudulent about the whole thing.

The lawyer, Galusha Parsons, went back home and started an investigation. Some incriminating facts were found that convinced Parsons the Cardiff Giant was made from Fort Dodge gypsum. He found that Hull had been registered in a local hotel and records showing the gypsum purchase. He even got the shipping route of the gypsum block showing it had gone to Chicago and then to Cardiff.

When word of this reached New York the corporation which now owned the giant denied the story. However, Hull, who had realized his profit from the venture and was now anxious for everyone to know how clever he had been, immediately admitted the whole thing.

Many people, especially the scientists who had been duped, were angry. Some refused to believe the giant wasn't real. But even more got a good laugh from the affair.

The popularity of the Cardiff Giant swiftly declined. It was later stored in a barn in the East and many years later exhibited in the Pan-American Exhibition in Buffalo, New York. It was shown several times at the Iowa State Fair and once was owned by Gardner Cowles of the *Des Moines Register* and *Tribune*. Now it is on display at the Farmers Museum in Cooperstown, New York.

The Cardiff Giant doesn't attract much attention today, but if it only had the gift of memory it could recall with satisfaction the days when it fooled scientists, amazed thousands of people, and made its owners rich men. And that's not bad for a cold block of Iowa gypsum.

25

The U.S.S. Iowa

It was noon on the 28th day of March, 1896, in a Philadelphia shipyard. A throng of people, many of them prominent in Washington, D. C., stood on the dock on the Delaware River admiring the keel of a giant ship which rested at an incline.

Then came a bark of command, a roar of engines, and the great hull started to move. Whistles blew and the crowd cheered as the daughter of the governor of Iowa, Mary Drake, smashed a bottle of champagne against the bow and shouted, "I christen thee Iowa."

A new national defender, the Iowa, was born.

The battleship Iowa had been authorized by an act of Congress on July 19, 1892, with an appropriation of $4,000,000.

By the time it was completed four years later the ship had rung up a bill of over $5,000,000. The resplendent red and white warship had an armor of plated steel, five great boilers and two sets of engines. She carried four 12-inch, eight 8-inch and six 4-inch guns and could pace a speed of sixteen knots an hour. Three hundred fifty feet long (longer than an average city block) and seventy-two feet wide, the Iowa was promptly hailed by newspapers as "Queen of Warships."

On June 16, 1897, the Iowa was put into commission with a crew of five hundred under command of Captain W. T. Sampson.

That same year a silver service, purchased with an appropriation of $5,000 by the Iowa General Assembly, was presented to the ship at Newport, Rhode Island.

The Iowa was initiated into action a year later during the Spanish-American War. She was stationed in a fleet outside the harbor of Santiago, Cuba, to blockade the entrance to the harbor. The fleet was spread out in a semicircle lest the enemy venture out.

On the morning of July 3, 1898, a Sunday, the Iowa broke the Sab-

The U.S.S. Iowa

bath calm with a shot from a small gun. This was a signal the enemy was trying to escape.

Immediately the American fleet sprang into action as the Spanish ships steamed out of the harbor. The Iowa first attacked the Teresa, firing two 12-inch shells that wrecked that vessel's steam pipes and took the lives of a number of crewmen. Then the Iowa turned its fire on two other enemy ships and soon put them out of commission.

When her fighting duties were over, the Iowa received on board two hundred fifty Spanish prisoners. The enemy captain unbuckled his sword belt as his men stood at attention, kissed the hilt of his sword and presented it to the victorious American commander, Captain Robley Evans. Captain Evans declined the sword but accepted the surrender and shook hands. The Iowa crew, blackened with powder and covered with perspiration, broke into cheers.

During the entire five-hour battle the American fleet lost only one man and had one serious casualty. The enemy's losses were estimated at three hundred twenty-three killed, one hundred fifty-one wounded and eighteen hundred prisoners.

For the next twenty years the career of the Iowa was quiet and uneventful. For several months preceding America's entrance into the first World War the ship was used as a receiving vessel. During the war she was assigned to coastal defense.

However, the years were taking their toll on the veteran and she was surpassed by new ships that were greatly improved. The Iowa was getting old and outdated. No longer was she "Queen of Warships."

The U.S.S. Iowa

In 1919 even the name Iowa was erased from the records and she was assigned the anonymous title of "B 54."

In March, 1923, almost exactly twenty-seven years after the ship was christened, the once-proud vessel met the fate of all ancient ships.

On the waters of the Pacific during naval spring maneuvers, preparations were made for the funeral of the Iowa. Surrounded by new and mighty ships, divested of her name, shorn of her crew and her flag, the warship was used as a target for the guns of the Mississippi, the new "Queen of the Navy."

Sailors on surrounding ships watched while great water spouts rose as shells struck the battered ship. As the echoes of the big guns died and the smoke cleared, the Iowa turned over and slipped below the blue waters.

The band of the Maryland struck up the Star Spangled Banner while fifteen thousand men of the surrounding fleet snapped into salute. As the waves closed over the smokestacks of the fallen Iowa, the Maryland fired the first volley of a twenty-one gun salute in final respect to the old battleship. Said Admiral Hiliary Jones, "She was a good ship."

PART FOUR

Brave Ones All

26

Rescue Mission to Spirit Lake

Often details surrounding exciting and well-known incidents in history are overlooked. For instance, one of the most dramatic episodes of the Spirit Lake massacre occurred when a rescue party, sent out to protect other settlers and bury the victims of the Spirit Lake tragedy, incurred untold hardships, suffering and death. This is the little-known story of a group of brave men who wrote a heroic sequel to Iowa's infamous Indian uprising.

Fort Dodge was stunned and rippling with excitement. Three bedraggled strangers had just arrived in town bearing news of a terrible massacre in the Spirit Lake-Okoboji region. The men said they had come across two cabins and discovered the terribly mutilated bodies of men, women and children, dead about two weeks. The date was March 22, 1857.

The shocking news aroused the settlers in Fort Dodge. Although no active troops remained in the city, Governor Grimes had authorized Major William Williams two years earlier to take any steps necessary to protect the northwestern Iowa residents from any Indian uprising. Major Williams, a veteran of many hard Iowa winters, feared that more killings might be in the making. He called for volunteers to form a relief expedition to forge across the snow-laden prairie and determine what had happened at Spirit Lake and offer protection to that area.

Major Williams warned the volunteers that the journey would be difficult and treacherous. How difficult, the Major and his some one hundred men would soon find out.

The news the three men brought to Fort Dodge was the first inkling that community had of Iowa's historic Spirit Lake massacre. Thirty-two people had been killed by the ruthless Inkpaduta and his band of rene-

RESCUE MISSION TO SPIRIT LAKE

gade Sioux. After roaming around the lake region murdering the settlers and looting their cabins early in March, 1857, the Sioux outlaws took thirteen-year-old Abigail Gardner and three women captive and set out northward to Springfield, Minnesota, to ravage another white settlement.

However, about the same time the relief expedition was starting out of Fort Dodge and Webster City, a trapper named Morris Markham reached Springfield and warned them of their peril. Markham had chanced upon the Okoboji area two days after the massacre started and slipped away without the Indians ever knowing of his presence. Thanks to his warning the Springfield residents joined together in a cabin and successfully resisted the attack when the Sioux came several days later.

The first night after the raid the besieged whites escaped the cabin and headed south. In this group was Eliza Gardner, sister of Abbie, who was visiting in Springfield at the time of the massacre. Eliza assumed her family were all dead and did not know of Abbie's kidnapping.

When Major Williams and his three companies left on their mission of mercy they did not know what had occurred in Spirit Lake or of the settlers fleeing toward them from Springfield. They did know their job would be a cold one.

The winter of 1856-57 had been the most severe on record and had not yet broken late in March. Sloughs and ravines were filled with snow in many places to a depth of six to fifteen feet. Sometimes the men waded through drifts waist high.

Despite the cold and the snow the men reached Dakota, in Humboldt County, the second night out. They were a hardy lot and included some men destined for fame. Among the party were C. C. Carpenter, who would later serve as governor of Iowa, and John F. Duncombe of Webster City who became one of Iowa's most prominent men and married Major Williams' daughter.*

On the third night the expedition had to camp on the unsheltered prairie on the snow. Without fuel and with a cold wind blowing down upon them they made a supper of crackers and raw pork and then crowded

---

*John F. Duncombe figures prominently in another story in this book, "The Death of Homer," Chapter 6.

together on the snow for warmth. A team of oxen and a wagon served as a windbreak.

On the morning of March 28, Major Williams addressed his men and told of the even greater hardships to come. He told them if they wanted to turn back, now was the time to do so. Only nine men left the ranks.

The rescue party reached the Irish colony of Emmetsburg and rested briefly. Here they were joined by some young men from the town. Since they were now deep in Indian territory the Major sent out nine men as scouts. About twelve miles north of Emmetsburg the scouts sighted the survivors of the Springfield attack.

Governor Carpenter, one of the scouts, later wrote:

. . . the women had worn out their shoes; their dresses were worn into fringe about the ankles; the children were crying with hunger and cold; the wounded were in deplorable condition . . . . Their food was entirely exhausted; their blankets were wet and frozen. If nothing more had been accomplished by the Relief Expedition, every member felt that the salvation of eighteen perishing refugees from almost certain death . . . had richly repaid them for all hardships encountered.

Major Williams led his men on toward Springfield until they reached the state line. Here they learned that a company of soldiers from Fort Ridgely was at Springfield for the protection of the settlers and that Inkpaduta and his redskins had moved on westward.

Since the danger to the settlers was over, the Major asked for twenty-five volunteers to go on to Spirit Lake as a burial detail while he took the remainder of his men back to Emmetsburg. On the second day of April, Captain J. C. Johnson led his party to the lakes to fulfill their grim mission.

The weather had started to warm as the men circled the lakes burying the dead. Not a living person in the whole region could be found. One member of the detail, Sergeant Hoover, told of a typical sight his men found upon entering a cabin:

There lay before us, in an incongruous heap, the mangled forms of seven human beings, from the aged grandmother down to the prattling child of tender years, who alike fell victims to the merciless savages' thirst for human blood.

Everywhere the men went they found bodies. One was lying in front of his cabin with a dead bulldog by his side. Both had been hacked to pieces. Another was found in the charred ruins of his cabin. Six mangled bodies were found outside the Gardner cabin.

The burial party started back to Emmetsburg on April 4 and ran into the most hazardous part of their journey. A cold wind started blowing that afternoon and by evening their clothes, which had gotten wet during the warm weather wading through sloughs, began to freeze.

By eight o'clock a raging blizzard was roaring over the prairie. The men floundered about wildly in the darkness while the mercury continued to plunge until it reached a low of thirty-four degrees below zero.

Two of the men, Captain Johnson and William Burkholder, who had recently been elected Webster County treasurer, became lost in the storm and perished. It was not until eleven years later that their skeletons were found.

As dawn broke the men found themselves in sight of timber on the Des Moines River. Some had to cut off their frozen boots and wrap their swollen feet in blankets for the rest of the journey. By the time the survivors reached the settlement many of the detachment were crawling on their hands and feet.

Years later, Captain Duncombe said of the relief expedition:

For severe hardships, continuing toil, constant exposure, bodily and mental suffering, I do not believe it has ever been surpassed— by men who have risked their lives to rescue their fellow men from peril and death."

27

Heroes of Harpers Ferry

WHEN John Brown made his bizarre raid on the government arsenal at Harpers Ferry, Virginia, in 1859, six of the original band of twenty-two men were Iowans. Two of these played roles in John Brown's fatal scheme that brought them action, adventure, honor and, for one, death on the gallows.

The men were brothers, Edwin and Barclay Coppoc, and their story reveals the great sympathy Iowans felt in the pre-Civil War days for the plight of the southern slaves. It also shows the faith many northerners placed in the fiery abolitionist, John Brown.

Edwin Coppoc was twenty-two and his brother, Barclay, only eighteen when John Brown visited their little Quaker village of Springdale, in Cedar County, in December, 1858. Brown was already well-known in the Midwest for his fight against slavery when he and his men stopped in town. Out of funds and tired, the group decided to spend the winter in Springdale. The Quakers hated slavery and welcomed Brown with open arms although they were careful to board the arms-bearing men with the Maxson family who were not Quakers.

The Coppoc brothers were very impressed with Brown. Although they had been raised in the Quaker faith by their widowed mother, both approved of the Kansan's violent methods to abolish slavery. The boys could be found daily with Brown at the Maxson farm.

During the long winter months the Iowans gained Brown's confidence. When the spring of 1859 came and the men had to leave, he told Edwin and Barclay to be ready to join him at a moment's notice as he was planning something big. Both agreed they would be eagerly awaiting his message.

In July the word came. Barclay told his mother, "We are going to start to Ohio today."

"Ohio," she exclaimed, not fooled by this intention to keep her from worrying. "I believe you are going with old Brown. When you get halters around your neck, will you think of me?"

"We cannot die in a better cause," Barclay replied.

Brown's plan was to take a select band of men and capture the government arsenal at Harpers Ferry, Virginia. The guns and ammunition obtained in the raid would be distributed to slaves and Brown thought a general uprising of all Negroes in the South would result.

Actually the plan was doomed from the start. Brown was putting a force of some twenty men against thirteen hundred inhabitants of Harpers Ferry, the government guards and the entire Virginia militia.

But on the Sunday night of October 16, 1859, the fantastic raid took place. By dark the men slipped into town and cut all telegraph wires. Edwin Coppoc was with Brown but Barclay and two others were left guarding the cabin outside of town that had been the gang's headquarters.

As dawn broke people began to appear on the streets, unaware of the intruders. They were taken prisoner and confined in a building in the armory yard. Some escaped though and spread the news of the attack. Within a few hours the whole countryside was aroused. They hurried to town, armed with whatever weapons they could muster.

Against unsurmountable odds the invaders did an amazing job of holding the Virginians at bay. The siege continued all day Monday, that night, and part of Tuesday. Then a squadron of United States Marines arrived under command of Colonel Robert E. Lee and the attack on Harpers Ferry was quelled.

When the smoke cleared most of Brown's men were dead or wounded. Edwin Coppoc and Brown were both captured and taken prisoner.

Edwin was put on trial and gained the respect of everyone for his quiet courage. On the 16th day of December young Coppoc and another prisoner sat on their coffins and rode in a farm wagon to a stubble field near Charles Town, Virginia. A black scaffold stood in the distance with a large crowd waiting around it.

After hoods were placed over their heads the two men shook hands and met their fate without flinching. John Brown was also hung for leading the raid at Harpers Ferry.

Barclay Coppoc and the two men left guarding their camp escaped when they learned of their companions' downfall. They started the long and dangerous journey northward to safety. The fugitives traveled mostly by night, raiding cornfields and chicken houses along the way for food.

The exhausted Barclay finally reached his home in Springdale on December 17, the day after his brother's execution.

But young Coppoc was not yet out of danger. Authorities from Virginia arrived in Des Moines the following year with extradition papers for the youth. Using a technical flaw in the document as an excuse to stall, Governor Kirkwood refused to honor the request. Messengers were then dispatched to Springdale to warn Barclay of his danger. He finally yielded to the pleas of his friends and went to Canada where he remained for several weeks.

Despite the harrowing experiences he had endured in his fight against slavery, Barclay Coppoc again yielded to the battle cry when the Civil War started. He joined the army and was commissioned a lieutenant in the Third Kansas Volunteer Infantry. His life came to a tragic end in a train wreck near St. Joseph, Missouri, caused by guerillas who had partially destroyed a bridge trestle.

Meanwhile northern troops were advancing southward singing "John Brown's Body" as they marched along. Cannons echoed throughout the land as men continued the fight for the cause in which John Brown and the Coppoc boys from Iowa had given their lives.

28

The Vote That Saved a President

"Senator Grimes, how say you?"

A hush fell over the United States Senate. All eyes were on Senator James Grimes of Iowa as he struggled to rise to cast his vote. His colleagues knew that Grimes was a sick man. He had suffered a light stroke a few days earlier and had been carried into the Senate chamber at the last minute for the roll call.

With great pain, the Senator pushed himself from his desk into an upright position. Despite his illness, Grimes' voice was strong. "Not guilty," he thundered.

The silence was broken as the Senators and spectators buzzed with excitement. Grimes collapsed back at his desk as the voting continued.

Tension mounted as the clerk finished the count and announced the result: thirty-five for conviction and nineteen for acquittal. By the lack of one vote from the required two-thirds majority, President of the United States Andrew Johnson was found not guilty of "high crimes and misdemeanors" and therefore not removed from office.

As the historic session ended, the Republican leaders were surprised and disappointed. The plan to oust Johnson, Abraham Lincoln's successor, had been in the making for months. Although a Republican, Johnson had alienated many members of his party with his generous attitude towards the South and reconstruction. He also was handicapped by a rather grim and tactless personality.

When the President suspended Lincoln's appointee, Secretary of War Stanton, the wrath of Congress fell upon him. The impeachment proceedings resulted.

The trial, with the United States Senate as jury and the Chief Justice of the Supreme Court as judge, started on March 5, 1868, and lasted until May 16.

A few days before the final vote, Senator Grimes announced that he did not feel the evidence was sufficient to convict Johnson of high crimes and misdemeanors, the constitutional grounds for removing a President from office.

Although Grimes did not care for Johnson or his administration, he felt the removal of a President would weaken our form of government. He said, "I cannot agree to destroy the harmonious working of the Constitution for the sake of getting rid of an unacceptable President."

Despite Grimes' announcement, the Republicans felt enough pressure could be brought upon him to change his mind. Iowa's other Senator, James Harlan, was given this task.

Two days before the final vote, Grimes suffered the stroke that was to put him under a physician's care. His friends did not believe he would be able to participate in the remainder of the session.

However, on the critical afternoon, the ailing Senator was carried into the packed Senate to his desk. Instead of using his illness to dodge the issue, the Iowan met it head-on.

After the vote, Grimes was severely criticized for his stand. The Republicans regarded him as a traitor. Old friends would not speak to him. His hometown paper printed a scathing editorial. The *New York Tribune* said of Grimes:

> *Those who know Mr. Grimes can easily understand why he—a Republican, raised to eminence by Republicans, trusted, honored, promoted, cherished by Republicans—seems compelled to send a Parthian arrow at the party life. History merely repeats itself. It seems that no generation can pass without giving us a man to live among the warnings of history; we have had Benedict Arnold, Aaron Burr, Jefferson Davis, and now we have James W. Grimes.*

The universal unpopularity of his position saddened Grimes, but he felt history would vindicate him. He never regained his health and resigned from the Senate in 1871. He died the following year at the age of fifty-five.

What is history's verdict of Grimes? Most historians feel the grounds for conviction of President Johnson were insufficient and his removal would have been a blow to the constitutional form of government. High praise is given to Grimes and the other eighteen Senators who had the courage to vote the way they honestly felt and could not be swayed by the tremendous pressure of public opinion.

Iowa, and the nation, can be proud that, in the midst of one of the most emotional and threatening periods of history, James Grimes added dignity, courage and statesmanship when it was needed most.

29

Heroine of the Bridge

As LONG as the lonesome rumble of trains winding their way over the Iowa prairie can be heard; and as long as railroad men gather to swap stories, the name of Kate Shelley will never be forgotten.

It has been over seventy years since fifteen-year-old Kate Shelley, daughter of a section hand who had been killed in an accident, ran two miles through wind and rain to warn an oncoming train of disaster ahead. Thanks to her bravery, what would have been one of Iowa's worst rail tragedies was averted. And Kate Shelley gained eternal fame.

The Shelley cabin was located in Boone County near the track of the Northwestern Railway. Honey Creek, ordinarily a small stream, winds its way through a forest near the Shelley cabin and empties into the Des Moines River not far from a railroad bridge near the town of Moingona. The cabin was located between the Honey Creek crossing and the large bridge leading into the station at Moingona.

On the stormy night of July 6, 1881, Kate and her mother were awakened by the crash of timbers and cries for help. Kate, over the protests of her mother, found a miner's lantern, made a wick from a piece of felt skirt, and went out into the night.

She found the Honey Creek bridge had collapsed and an engine sent out to inspect the track was in the raging water. The engineer and brakeman were clinging to an uprooted tree on the other side of the creek. The engineer yelled to Kate that they were safe but the midnight express was soon due to cross the fallen bridge.

Kate did not hesitate. Turning towards Moingona and clutching her lantern she started off for the station to warn the oncoming express.

Through the blinding darkness and driving rain the girl followed the track through the forest. Many times she stumbled and cut her legs on the rough ties. The lantern was soon extinguished by the rain. Yet the brave teenager went on.

Finally she reached the trestle over the Des Moines River. The bridge was five hundred feet long with rails resting on crossties several feet apart. There was no floor to the structure.

Mustering her remaining strength, Kate started the perilous crossing. It was impossible for her to stand up because of the fierce wind so she got down on her hands and knees.

The tempest was now at its worst. The timbers were wet and slippery; the rain was blinding and the gale threatened to blow Kate from the trestle. One slip and she would plunge into the raging torrent below. There also was the danger that the express might come at any moment.

But Kate Shelley crossed the bridge and ran the remaining half-mile to the Moingona station. The startled agent flashed the message over the telegraph and the train was warned before it crossed the fatal trestle.

When the train stopped at Moingona the passengers gathered around the little Irish girl to thank her for saving them from certain death.

As word spread of Kate's deed the nation's press picked up the story and the whole country was thrilled by her bravery. The name of Kate Shelley was known everywhere and she was hailed in stories and poems as "The Heroine of the Bridge."

The Northwestern Railway gave Kate a financial gift and the *Chicago Tribune* presented a purse that took care of the mortgage on the Shelley home. In 1926 a bridge across the Des Moines River was built near Moingona and named in Kate's honor.

Kate, who never married, in later life accepted the railroad's offer of a lifetime job as Moingona station agent. She died in 1912. The lantern, with a broken glass, is now in the State Historical Museum in Des Moines.

Throughout Kate's life, the modest woman was proudest of a gold medal awarded after her famous journey by the Iowa General Assembly. Inscribed on the medal were the words:

KATE SHELLEY
—whom neither the terror of elements
nor the fear of death could appall in
her efforts to save human lives.

30

The Five Sullivans

On December 7, 1941, the Tom Sullivan family was listening to the radio in their comfortable Waterloo, Iowa, home.

Suddenly their regular Sunday afternoon program was interrupted by a network announcer who told the frightening news of the Japanese attack on Pearl Harbor. War was imminent.

Mrs. Sullivan started crying softly and looked at her five sons. George, the oldest, stood up and said, "Well, I guess our minds are made up, aren't they, fellows? And when we go in, we want to go in together. If the worst comes to worst, why we'll all have gone down together."

These words proved prophetic.

Without hesitating, the five Sullivan brothers—Joseph, twenty-three, Matt, twenty-two, Al, nineteen, Frank, twenty-five, and George, twenty-seven—enlisted in the United States Navy. Frank and George had already spent four years in that service.

At the time of their enlistment all were employed at the Rath Packing Company in Waterloo. Only Al, the "baby" of the family, was married and had a son.

The brothers were sent to the Great Lakes, Illinois, Naval Training Station for their preliminary training. When this was completed they were all assigned to the U.S.S. Juneau, a new light cruiser that owned the distinction of being the first warship commissioned in camouflage.

In assigning the brothers to the same ship the Navy was breaking a long-standing policy of dividing up brother teams. The reason for this is obvious; that in the case of a ship's sinking a family would not have more than one casualty aboard. This policy was ignored in the case of the Sullivans for one reason. When they enlisted they insisted they did so on the condition they be together at all times. The Navy was honoring its commitment in allowing the brothers to remain together.

The Five Sullivans

The Sullivan boys enjoyed sea life and wrote many letters home to their parents telling of the war and their sea duties. Then in the fall of 1942 the letters stopped coming.

From November through the dreary winter months the Sullivans received no news of their sons. The family became increasingly worried and fear for the Sullivans' safety became a major concern of Waterloo. The family priest and friends prayed for the boys.

Then on an icy January 12, 1943, a special representative of the United States Navy arrived in Waterloo bearing the news that the whole community dreaded to hear. He informed the parents that their five sons had perished on November 13, 1942, when the gallant U.S.S. Juneau was sunk off the Solomon Islands during an enemy attack.

The Five Sullivans

As the news spread the entire state grieved with the family over the enormity of their loss. Gold Star mothers who had lost one son in the fighting could well imagine the blow to a mother who lost all five. Newspapers proclaimed the tragedy in headlines as reporters and newsreel cameramen swarmed into Waterloo. The post office used extra men to handle the volume of mail Americans sent the saddened parents. Twice the President of the United States, Franklin Roosevelt, wrote the family.

The "Five Sullivans" became a symbol of all men fighting and dying for their country. Instead of plunging into despair the parents showed the same kind of bravery that ran in their sons and set out to do all they could to keep the memory of their boys alive. Mr. and Mrs. Sullivan gave speeches at shipyards, defense plants, bond rallies and launched new ships. One vessel they christened was named after their sons. The "Five Sullivans" became a new rallying cry for Americans.

The tributes to the Sullivans rolled in. Hollywood produced a movie about them and it played to hundreds of thousands. The family became subjects of radio shows, plays and dozens of magazine articles.

A group called the "Sullivans of America" collected enough money to erect a statue of the Virgin Mary on the lawn of St. Mary's Catholic Church in Waterloo. The *Waterloo Daily Courier* announced a fund drive which netted $7,000 for a memorial hospital ward. Maxwell Park in Waterloo was renamed Sullivan Park.

For the duration of the war the name Sullivan inspired Americans. Even after the fighting was over the boys were not forgotten. In 1952, ten years after they lost their lives on the ill-fated Juneau, officials dedicated a row of apple trees on the capitol lawn in Washington, D. C., to the memory of the Five Sullivans. A grateful nation could never forget the great sacrifice made by this Iowa family.

During the Civil War President Lincoln wrote Mrs. Bixby, whom he understood had lost five sons in that fighting, words that might just as easily apply to Mr. and Mrs. Sullivan:

I pray that our Heavenly Father may assuage the anguish of your bereavement, and leave you only the cherished memory of the loved and lost, and the solemn pride that must be yours, to have laid so costly a sacrifice upon the altar of Freedom.

(Author's Note: As a matter of historical accuracy it should be noted that President Lincoln was incorrectly informed by the War Department of the extent of Mrs. Bixby's loss. Two of her sons had died, one was taken prisoner at Gettysburg and later returned safely. One boy deserted to the Confederacy and another was discharged by the Army but went to sea as a sailor.)

PART FIVE

Writers, Artists and Dreamers

31

The Man Without a Poem

UNDERNEATH a large shade tree in the little northeastern Iowa town of Delhi rests a simple granite marker erected to the memory of a poet. It isn't a large marker, nor is it particularly impressive, but it does commemorate in death the work of a man who was ignored in life.

In fact, the man in whose memory this monument was built was not only ignored, he was rebuffed, repulsed, laughed at, criticized, and called a fool for thirty years. When he died he went to his grave a disheartened and disillusioned man. For it was his unhappy fate to have written a poem—a poem that became famous in every corner of the world but which was always credited to another author.

The strange and lonely saga of John Luckey McCreery began on a starry winter night in 1863. McCreery was a young man of twenty-eight who had drifted into Delhi and purchased the *Delaware County Journal*. The weekly was heavily mortgaged and his financial difficulties caused the young editor to be in a pensive mood as he returned home late one night behind a plugging horse.

As McCreery rode along the Delaware County countryside the beauty of the winter night inspired him and he found a poem bubbling up inside him. "There is no death, there is no death"—over and over this phrase sprang from within McCreery's soul. Soon the first stanza of a poem was shaped on the Iowa prairie.

> There is no death! The stars go down
>   To rise upon some other shore
> And bright in heaven's jeweled crown
>   They shine for evermore.

One by one the words and the cadence fell into place as the young editor rode on. By the time he reached Delhi, McCreery had conceived most of the poem and immediately set it down on paper back in his newspaper office. He titled his work "There Is No Death" and when it was finished there were ten stanzas. Then he put the manuscript in a desk drawer and went home to bed.

If John McCreery had left his poem in the desk drawer his later years might have been much more peaceful. But he didn't. Instead, in February or March, 1863, the budding poet resurrected "There Is No Death," put a few polishing touches on it and mailed it to *Arthur's Home Magazine,* a popular journal of that time. A long, involved and confusing tale of anguish was on its way.

The editors at the magazine liked the poem and published it in their July, 1863, issue. This pleased McCreery immensely and he reprinted it in his own paper and quite a few other weeklies followed suit.

Then one Eugene Bulmer of Dixon, Illinois, came into the picture. Bulmer, a frustrated author himself, saw "There Is No Death" in his local paper and incorporated it into an article he was writing on immortality. When he finished his piece he left off McCreery's name, signed his own with a flourish, and sent it off to the *Farmers Advocate* in Chicago which printed it.

Although the situation was now considerably mixed up, another newspaper editor added his bit to make things worse. This unknown editor liked the poem and ran it in his own sheet. But when he saw the by-line "Bulmer" he decided this must be a misprint, that the author was probably Bul*W*er, and changed the credit to "F. Bulwer, Lord of Lytton," a famous English poet. Poor J. L. McCreery was lost in the shuffle.

Soon the poem caught on with the public and started popping up here and there, always credited to Bulwer. The hapless McCreery, who by this time had lost his paper and was working on a Dubuque daily, often saw his poem with the Bulwer by-line and became enraged. He fired off letter after letter to editors of various publications but they wrote him off as a crackpot.

And "There Is No Death" became more and more popular. It was reprinted in newspapers all over the world, in song books, school readers and magazines. Burton Stevenson, in his book *Famous Single Poems*, wrote that it was ". . . the sort of poem which orators on the Chautauqua circuit love to spout and literary societies of Gopher Prairie to recite and obituary writers of the country press to quote." It was said that no congressman could be buried properly without "There Is No Death" being recited at his bier. Stevenson states that no other poem in the English language has been spoken so often above an open grave.

As the poem's fame grew, McCreery stepped up his campaign to be recognized as its author. But he met with little success. One reason for this was probably due to McCreery's dreamy, impractical nature. He seemed unable to get along well in the world and could never hold a job of much importance. He also harbored vague and grandiose schemes for the betterment of mankind that he just never got around to.

But despite his failings, John McCreery *was* the true author and the injustice of his plight would be enough to sear the soul of even a more stable person. Then, to make the poet's burden even greater, he actually lost out on a job because of his literary work.

This occurred in 1868 when President Ulysses S. Grant returned to his hometown of Galena, Illinois, for a visit. McCreery's friends had recommended him for the position of White House stenographer and

The Man Without a Poem

appeared to present their case in person. Grant seemed about ready to give McCreery the job when one of the poet's friends pulled out "There Is No Death" and proudly read it to the President. Grant listened, thought a moment and then shook his head. No, it might be a good poem, he reasoned, he was no judge of that. But it was his experience that a man good at making poems was not much good for anything else. McCreery didn't get the job.

Although discouraged, McCreery did eventually get an appointment as a stenographer for the Committee on Indian Affairs in Washington, D. C. He lived quietly with his family in the capital city the remainder of his life, always continuing his letter barrage to editors trying to establish his claim to the now famous poem.

McCreery's greatest success came in 1875 when Harper Brothers changed one of their school readers and gave him credit for the poem after five years of debate and investigation. Another milestone was reached in 1889 when *Lippincott's Magazine* ran a series called "One Hundred Questions" concerning literary matters and, after due consideration, pronounced McCreery the real author of "There Is No Death."

These glimmers of success were bright but not enough. McCreery kept up his fight until 1906 when he died following an appendicitis operation in Duluth, Minnesota. He is buried in Washington, D. C. McCreery's only other work during his lifetime was a collection of verses called *Songs of Toil and Triumph* released in 1883. It wasn't much of a success.

The night before McCreery died he wrote a "last message" to the world. He said:

My only regret is that all the great work I have always contemplated doing for humanity remains undone. The bread and butter necessities of life have prevented my getting to it.

Upon his death the *Delaware County Journal,* the paper which he once owned, in the town of Delhi, where he wrote his world-famous poem, saw fit to give only a half-dozen lines to the life and death of John Luckey McCreery.

THERE IS NO DEATH

John Luckey McCreery

There is no death! The stars go down
    To rise upon some other shore
And bright in heaven's jeweled crown
    They shine for evermore.

There is no death! The dust we tread
    Shall change beneath the summer showers
To golden grain or mellow fruit
    Or rainbow-tinted flowers.

The granite rocks disorganize
    To feed the hungry moss they bear;
The forest leaves drink daily life
    From out the viewless air.

There is no death! The leaves may fall,
    The flowers may fade and pass away—
They only wait, through wintry hours,
    The coming of the May.

There is no death! An angel form
    Walks o'er the earth with silent tread;
He bears our best-loved things away
    And then we call them "dead."

He leaves our hearts all desolate—
    He plucks our fairest, sweetest flowers;
Transplanted into bliss, they now
    Adorn immortal bowers.

The bird-like voice, whose joyous tones
   Made glad this scene of sin and strife,
Sings now an everlasting song
   Amid the tree of life.

Where'er He sees a smile too bright,
   Or soul too pure for taint or vice,
He bears it to that world of light,
   To dwell in Paradise.

Born unto that undying life,
   They leave us but to come again;
With joy we welcome them—the same
   Except in sin and pain.

And ever near us, though unseen,
   The dear immortal spirits tread;
For all the boundless universe
   Is life—there are no dead!

32

Iowa's Wild West Writer

The Iowan who killed more redskins and brought the strong arm of justice to more badmen than any other man in the state did so with his pen and not a flintlock.

He was Oll Coomes, an Iowa farmer who became one of the most prolific writers of the sensational dime thrillers that were so very popular in the late 1800's.

Oll Coomes lived on a farm about three miles southeast of Wiota in Cass County. At night, after he had toiled all day on his one-hundred-sixty-acre farm, Coomes would sit at his redwood desk in the front room of the big frame farmhouse and conjure up stories of murderous and bloodthirsty Indians, mean-tempered and treacherous outlaws and their undoing by noble and courageous cavalry men.

He would set these tales down on paper, give them such titles as *Hawkeye Harry, the Young Trapper Ranger, Vagabond Joe, Delaware Dick, Minkskin Mike, Webfoot Mose, Blundering Basil,* and *Tiger Tom, the Texas Terror,* and then send them off to the Beadle Publishing Company in New York City.

For most of his works Coomes received $50 to $100, but his *Omaha, Prince of the Prairie,* brought the then-fabulous price of $1,000. These stories sold by the thousands all over the nation.

Coomes' adventures were packed with excitement and red-blooded action. Although some doubts have been cast as to their historical accuracy, no one could deny the suspense and interest of a Coomes thriller.

Take the case of the young trapper, Hawkeye Harry, one of Coomes' favorite characters. Harry lived in northeastern Iowa with his sidekick, Old Optic, and was dubbed Hawkeye because he sported a cap made from the skin of a hawk with wings on the side.

Hawkeye and Old Optic never farmed or spent their time as most pioneers of the 1800's. Instead they bounced around from adventure to adventure—rescuing beautiful Nora Gardette, a maiden of "exquisite loveliness," from all kinds of peril, and bringing a justice to Rat Rangle and his band of outlaws.

One predicament the young trapper found himself in took place as he was crossing a chasm called Black Gorge. Our hero was carefully balancing his way on a fallen tree when he met face to face with an Indian halfway across.

Both men dropped to a sitting position, entwined their legs around the log and started fighting. To and fro they swayed and battled on the creaking log over the deep abyss. Then both slipped and turned upside down—still fighting. As Coomes described it:

Half-strangled, the redskin loosened his hold upon the youth's body, and becoming dizzy and faint, with a determined effort to drag the youth down into the abyss with him, he clutched the lad with both hands by the throat as his feet slipped apart; but unable to maintain the hold upon the throat, with a wild despairing shriek that echoed in prolonged wails through the gorge, the doomed wretch went whizzing down into the fearful abyss.

But Harry was not out of danger yet! Tired and dazed, dangling upside down over the ravine, he heard someone approaching him on the log. More Indians? No! Thank heavens it was Old Optic, who pulled Harry to safety and observed: "That war a ticklish place, Hawkeye."

Stories such as this made the Iowa author one of the most popular and sought after western writers of his day. In all, Coomes turned out over one hundred thrillers. Although he received many offers to move east and write or edit the pulp magazines, Coomes refused, saying he preferred life on his Iowa farm.

Although the author wrote as if he knew and lived adventure, his life was quiet. Coomes traveled very little and had never visited any of the western scenes he wrote about until many years after his books were things of the past. Coomes died violently, however, in an automobile accident near Storm Lake in 1921 at the age of seventy-six.

The farmhouse near Wiota is still owned by members of the author's family. The old redwood desk where Oll Coomes breathed life into Reckless Rollo, Antelope Abe and dozens of other exciting characters occupies a prized place in the old homestead.

33

Bob Burdette, Homespun Humorist

WHAT Will Rogers was to the nation in the 1930's, Bob Burdette was to Iowa in the 1880's. Writer, lecturer, homespun philosopher, Bob Burdette was one of this state's most popular men and his sunny outlook on life spread cheer throughout Iowa. His daily column on the pages of the *Burlington Hawk Eye* was quoted and discussed in thousands of homes all over the Midwest.

Robert J. "Bob" Burdette was not an Iowan by birth. He first saw the light of day in Greene County, Pennsylvania, a "county just big enough to be born in." His family came to Illinois a few years later and Bob attended school in Peoria. After graduation he enlisted in the infantry and later returned to Peoria and taught school, living on the family farm. However, he did not like farm life, saying the custom was "to go to bed at sunset, get up in the night as though the sun did not know when to start the day." These early rising hours probably led to his famous remark later that, "The early bird might get the worm, but think how much better the worm would have been if he had stayed in bed."

Burdette got a job with the Peoria paper and started his humorous style of writing. He left a few years later when the managing editor expressed displeasure over the amusing slant his jolly reporter worked into all his news accounts. In reporting on a revival he had attended, Burdette described how the crowd was packed together and the emotional impact engulfed all present. ". . . had the usher trod on the corns of the man at the end of the seat I believe all the rest of us would have hollered."

After leaving Peoria, Bob Burdette came to Burlington and joined the *Hawk Eye* staff. When he arrived the paper was a small, conservative daily with a short list of subscribers. Upon his departure fourteen years later, the *Hawk Eye* was one of the liveliest, most influential publications in the state with readers in every state in the Union.

Bob Burdette, Homespun Humorist

It wasn't long before Burdette was the most popular writer in Iowa and was given a column all his own to tell of the daily doings of such fictional characters as the Middlerib and Bilderback families.

One of Burdette's most popular columns told of the picnic the Middlerib family had planned for weeks. On the big day "just one little cloud" poured rain on the gathering and much confusion followed. Aunt Carrie left the baby under the table as they ran for shelter, the cat got his head in the cream jar and it became stuck "tight as wax," and old Mr. Rubelking lost his teeth in the coffee pot. Then as the disheveled and tired group dragged home they were met by callers, "the most fashionable people in town."

Along with his accounts of the misadventures of the Middleribs, Burdette's wise sayings were widely quoted. "Bob Burdette says—" was often heard among groups of farmers discussing local politics or crops in Iowa's little towns. Mothers would repeat his comments to the children, hoping to impart to them some of Bob's wisdom.

Among his bits of philosophy were such items as: "I have known men so great they were of no account. You have seen trees so big you couldn't tie a horse to them," and "It is easier to be great than it is to be humble." Burdette always said, "Humor is but the garment of truth."

Along with his newspaper work, Burdette started lecturing on the Chautauqua circuit and was a great success. He continued his writing by letters signed "Roaming Robert," recounting his adventures in traveling the Midwest. His most famous speech concerned the "Rise and Fall of the Mustache."

In 1888 Burdette left Iowa for California because of his wife's health. Ten years later he entered the ministry of the Baptist Church. Burdette said that anyone who thought he was giving up newspaper work for the less strenuous life of a preacher was wrong. He compared the life of a minister to that of ". . . falling downstairs with a kitchen stove or dodging automobiles on racing day."

From 1903 to 1914, "Roaming Robert," now known as "Reverend Burdette," served as pastor of the Temple Baptist Church in Los Angeles. Upon his death in 1914 the whole state mourned the passing of Iowa's favorite humorist.

34

America's Waltz King

On the lawn of a fine old home in Oskaloosa stands a monument that pays tribute to an Iowan who once lived in that house and spent his time writing songs. And the songs this man wrote became so popular that he became well-known throughout the country, mingled with the famous in the musical world and in the twilight of his career was hailed as "America's Waltz King."

Frederick Knight Logan was destined by fate to become a musician. Born in Oskaloosa in 1871, Logan became the sole pride and joy of his musical mother, Virginia Knight Logan. Mrs. Logan, who became a widow when Frederick was very young, was a talented coloratura soprano opera singer and teacher of voice and harmony.

Mrs. Logan frequently went on tours with different companies and when Frederick became older he accompanied his mother. During these trips Frederick began to develop an interest in music. Encouraged and trained by his mother, young Logan seriously took up the study of music.

After graduating from Oskaloosa High School, Logan attended the College of Music in Chicago and studied under professional teachers in New York.

At the completion of his formal schooling, the budding musician was hired as musical director for the David Henderson Productions. This company performed all over the country and engaged local musicians to supplement the orchestra. Logan's job was to train these hometown musicians and whip them into shape before the opening performance. It is said that Logan conducted orchestras in practically every large city in the country.

Later Logan worked for Jefferson de Angeles' Opera Company and then he received his first important position as musical director for Montgomery and Stone's New York production of "The Wizard of Oz."

Next David Belasco hired him away as director for his theater and then Logan traveled from coast to coast in Maude Adams' repertoire of "Peter Pan." He also wrote musical scores for Chauncy Olcott.

But after a few seasons the strain of constant travel and opening night pressure wearied Logan and he gave up his demanding career to return to Iowa. He went back to Oskaloosa and made his home with his mother. Here they established the "Knight-Logan Studios of Musical Art" and gave voice, harmony and piano lessons to students from far and near.

Courtesy, Des Moines Register
Frederick Knight Logan

In the peace and quiet of a small town, Frederick Knight Logan composed the song that made him famous. One story has it that an orchestra leader who traveled the Midwest appeared one day at Logan's home and hummed parts of a tune that he had heard in Missouri. Logan took the tune, arranged and rearranged it and finally came up with a polished composition he called "The Missouri Waltz." Immediately this work became one of America's favorite waltzes and earned Logan a handsome income for the rest of his life.

Besides "The Missouri Waltz," Logan wrote such beautiful songs as "Pale Moon," "Fallen Leaf" and "Blue Rose Waltz." As the years went by and his tunes continued to grow in popularity, Frederick Knight Logan was called "America's Waltz King." He received many offers to return to theater work but he refused all, saying he preferred life in Iowa to the confusion and distractions of the city.

Personally, Logan was regarded with both affection and awe in his hometown. Some residents who remember him describe the composer as "rather odd" and a "lone wolf" but all agree that he had a "cheerful disposition." Logan and his mother had a large collection of phonograph records that Frederick liked to play at top volume. Often he would invite friends into his home to listen to his musical collection.

Logan never married and continued to live with his aged mother until death cut short his brilliant career on June 11, 1928, at the age of fifty-seven. Mrs. Logan lived until the early 1940's. Now both mother and son are buried in Oskaloosa's Forest Cemetery.

Today, over three decades after his death, the main income of the Oskaloosa Women's Club is derived from royalties earned by "The Missouri Waltz"—the unforgettable song by Frederick Knight Logan, "America's Waltz King."

(Author's Note: The orchestra leader mentioned here was later identified by Earl Hall of the *Mason City Globe-Gazette* as John Eppel of Boone who traveled the Midwest with a very popular dance orchestra in the 1910-1920 decade.

Eppel is reported to have heard a Negro custodian of an Elks Club tapping out a melody with one finger on a piano. The orchestra leader liked the tune and his band used it on many occasions.

Logan took the melody, polished it up and copyrighted the song. Most musical records credit Logan with the composition of "The Missouri Waltz" but some list John Eppel as the composer.)

35

Jack London and Kelly's Army

In April and May of 1894 an Army that never fired a shot or fought a battle passed through Iowa on its way to Washington, D. C. Among the some two thousand footsore volunteers was a handsome, nineteen-year-old boy who was joyously soaking in the hardship and adventure that would later help him pen tales of the road and the wild that were to make him famous. The Army was known as "Kelly's Industrial Army" and the boy was Jack London.

Kelly's Army was an army in name only. It was composed of young drifters and vagrants looking for excitement and a number of older, unemployed men. Its leader was "General" Charles Kelly who had formed the movement in the West to travel to the nation's capital to convince Congress it should pass a public works project to aid unemployment. Kelly planned to join Coxey's Army which started out from Ohio for the same purpose and received nationwide attention.

General Kelly arrived in Iowa in April and camped for a time in Chautauqua Park in Council Bluffs. Although they had come much of the way by train their numbers had increased to the point where the railroad would not provide transportation. So, Kelly decided to walk his Army to Washington.

They left Council Bluffs on April 19 with twelve wagons loaded with gear and the General leading the way astride a fine black horse given him by local supporters. The marchers carried American flags, posters and banners, many of which proclaimed "Kelly for President."

The first night out in Iowa the weather pulled a surprise and turned cold and rainy. The men found lodging wherever they could, mostly in barn haylofts. The owner of an elevator gave permission for the men to use it and before midnight the huge structure was crammed with three hundred men.

Iowa was friendly to the Army. When they would pass through a town the entire population would turn out to cheer the boys on. If they camped overnight an afternoon ball game would be arranged between the Army nine and the local town team; community sings would be held and the whole town would move out to the camp grounds for speeches and visiting. A holiday atmosphere would take over the community.

The men found the Iowans generous. Many times they were met along the way by farmers with freshly slaughtered steers and farm wives carrying baskets of homemade bread. Storekeepers even gave handouts to the Army. Since their provisions were quite low the offerings were gratefully accepted.

Kelly led his men through Neola, Minden, Avoca, Walnut, Marne, Atlantic and then along the route of Highway 6 through Wiota, Anita, Adair, Casey, Stuart and Dexter. On April 30 they reached Des Moines and were greeted by a large crowd as they trudged through the city. The Army made camp at a vacant stove works located about a mile east of the state capitol.

Kelly decided to let his men rest in Des Moines to gain wind for the rest of the journey. The Salvation Army set up shop and gave the men coffee and held religious services on the grounds. In the afternoons the Army boys played ball with Des Moines youths. Usually the visitors won. For the most part Des Moines citizens enjoyed the Army's stay and found them "gentlemanly and mannerly."

However, officials were worried lest the men become permanent settlers and tried to talk the railroads into moving them to the next stop. The rail companies refused. Des Moines residents then pitched in and took up a fund to pay expenses to build rafts to float down the Des Moines River.

This proved successful and after eight days of encampment the Army said farewell to Iowa's capital city and started down the river.

Jack London was a stocky, well built young man with curly hair and a thirst for adventure and action. He had been a hobo and a sailor in his young life and latched onto the Kelly movement more for the sake of the trip than for any social or economic reason. However, his contacts with people from all walks of life and the hardships he encountered were to have a profound effect on his later writing.

London kept a complete diary of his day by day activities with Kelly. He told of sleeping in the loft of a large barn in western Iowa when a cat with a litter of kittens crawled into the hay. One of the men sleeping there wanted to toss the cats outside but Jack protested, telling him before he threw the cats out he would have to throw him out too. London and the cats all stayed.

On the tramp from Council Bluffs, London's shoes were worn through the soles and his feet became covered with blisters. Vowing he could not walk another step, the boy laid down on the street of Avoca as the Army passed around him. Later the city marshal came by and told him to move on. After explaining his plight, the marshal overtook the Army and made two officers come back to town and pick up London in a wagon.

The youth enjoyed most his stay in Des Moines where he let his blistered feet heal. After taking the boats downstream, London and his fellow crewmen left Kelly and went their own way.

General Kelly pushed on to Washington with only a few remaining followers. There they found General Coxey in jail for walking on the grass. Discouraged, they disbanded and returned home.

Jack London went on to write such favorite novels as *White Fang* and *Call of the Wild*, which were to place his name in the roster of the great writers of all time. He continued his adventurous living and writing until taking his own life in 1916.

36

American Gothic

THE house that serves as a background in one of America's most famous paintings still stands in Eldon, Iowa, just as it was painted over three decades ago.

The painting is by Iowa's best-known artist, Grant Wood, and is known around the world as "American Gothic." The name was derived from the second floor Gothic window of the Iowa home.

Grant Wood was born in Anamosa but spent most of his life in Cedar Rapids and Iowa City. His career as an artist had been quite unsuccessful until one day in 1930 when he happened to see the house with the oblong window in Eldon. The lines of the home appealed to him and he visualized the portrait of a farming couple with the house in the background.

After having a friend take a snapshot of the house with a box camera, Wood searched for the right faces for the farming couple. He selected his sister, Nan, and his dentist, Dr. B. H. McKeeby of Cedar Rapids. Dr. McKeeby was very reluctant to pose for the painting and did so only after Grant assured him that he would not be recognized.

The actual painting took three months. The sittings were done in Wood's studio in Cedar Rapids which was furnished him rent free by a friendly mortician who also displayed the artist's pictures in his establishment.

Grant dressed Dr. McKeeby in a dress shirt, overalls, and a suit coat. He wanted him to resemble a farmer "who might be a preacher on Sunday." Nan wore her mother's cameo and an apron that Grant had picked out of a mail-order catalog and ordered from Chicago.

When the painting was finished, Wood sold his work for $300, a good price then, to the Chicago Art Institute where it hangs today. When it was displayed at the Institute's annual exhibition in 1930, "American

American Gothic

Gothic" became the hit of the show. People crowded in long lines to get a glimpse of the painting by this unknown Iowa artist.

"An Iowa Moses," the critics hailed Wood and acclaimed him as the art world's newest discovery. Overnight, Grant Wood was famous.

But Dr. McKeeby was unhappy with the masterpiece. He was an affable, friendly person and didn't like being portrayed to the world as a stern, grim farmer. And despite Grant's promise, the dentist was easily recognizable.

For over five years Dr. McKeeby would not admit he had posed for the picture. When asked about it he would reply "What do you think?" or "It could be, I suppose." Finally, in 1935, he publicly announced his role.

After "American Gothic" had become nationally famous it was exhibited in Cedar Rapids. Nan and Dr. McKeeby were asked to stand beside the painting for a photograph but the dentist at first refused. Finally he acceded and posed with the painting that had made his face known throughout the country.

In answer to some critics who felt the couple represented a too-grim picture of farm life, Wood said his work portrayed a small-town couple, not farmers. Questioners then asked why the man in the painting was holding a pitchfork if he lived in town. Wood also said the couple were father and daughter, not man and wife.

Despite scattered protests by farmers, "American Gothic" gained steadily in fame and popularity. In 1941 *Fortune* magazine suggested it be made into a war poster with "government of the people, by the people and for the people" printed underneath.

When Grant Wood died on February 12, 1942, at the age of fifty-one, "American Gothic" was acclaimed his greatest work.

The house, with its famous Gothic window now covered with plastic to keep out the Iowa wind, stands a few blocks from Main Street in Eldon, a town of thirteen hundred southeast of Ottumwa.

For over twenty years the landmark, owned by Mrs. Eldon Smith of Batavia, has been occupied by Mrs. P. W. Smith who reports visitors still drive by the home every summer. It needs a coat of paint now and a few repairs here and there, but otherwise it looks just like it did over three decades ago when Grant Wood painted his way to immortality.

PART SIX

A Few Assorted Characters

37

Abner Kneeland's Dream Colony

In May of 1839 a kindly, white-haired man of sixty-five got off the boat at Fort Madison. Although he looked his years the man stepped with a spring and his eyes glowed with the zeal of a man with a mission. The old gentleman's name was Abner Kneeland and he was destined to leave his mark on the pages of Iowa's history.

Abner Kneeland was a New Englander whose life had been a whirlwind of controversy and turmoil. Although a Baptist, Kneeland had begun to question his church's beliefs as early as 1803 and was about to be tried for heresy when he united with the Universalists. He became an ordained minister in this faith in 1805 and preached in New Hampshire. During this time he also served in the state legislature and wrote a book on spelling reform.

For several years the energetic minister was contented but his doubting mind eventually led him to question his own faith. He suspended himself from the ministry in 1829, saying,

> ... *it is my desire ... to suspend myself as to fellowship of the order until I shall be able to give entire satisfaction that the cause of the World's Redeemer ... of God, of truth and righteousness ... is the cause in which I am laboring and to which my talents are devoted.*

After leaving his church Kneeland and his wife went to Boston and founded a publication known as the *Boston Investigator*. In 1833 his writing brought down a furor. Kneeland declared that he did not believe the story of Christ, and he had no faith in miracles or in the resurrection.

These words, uttered in old New England, were considered slightly worse than treason and Abner Kneeland was indicted under the Massachusetts law for blasphemy.

During the trial that followed Kneeland pled to the jury:

I had no occasion to deny that there was a God. I believe that the whole universe is nature and that God and nature are synonymous terms. I believe in a God that embraces all power, wisdom, justice, and goodness. Everything is God.

But this sentiment failed to persuade the jury and the former preacher was convicted and sentenced to sixty days in jail.

The imprisonment of a man for merely expressing his own opinion was criticized all over the country. Many newspapers came to Kneeland's defense. As far away as Iowa the Dubuque paper thundered:

Abner Kneeland, editor of the Boston Investigator, *on the anniversary of the battle of Bunker Hill, was lodged in jail, there doomed to sixty days' confinement, for the exercise of that privilege to gain which the heroes of the revolution shed their blood, sixty-three years before, on the hill in plain view from the window of his prison cell.*

Upon his release from prison, Kneeland decided it was time to find a land where freedom of ideas and speech were respected. In fact, he wanted to establish a colony of men and women like himself, people with inquiring minds. A community with no church or minister around to "air his superstitions." And where would be a better place to start such a colony than in the new frontier territory of Iowa?

The result of Kneeland's dreams was a little settlement located near Farmington, in Van Buren County, and christened Salubria. Kneeland built a two-story home for his family and served as leader for the several families who were attracted to the town. He sometimes performed marriage ceremonies in the front of his home.

Kneeland thrived in his new surroundings and liked Iowa. After enjoying dinner at the home of another settler he wrote back East:

For aught I can see to the contrary there may be as much independence enjoyed in a log cabin with such a dinner as we had yesterday—fresh pork and chickens, new potatoes and green peas—as in a palace with all the dainties and luxuries which can be found at the tables of the great dons of our cities.

Another time he hailed Iowa as a land "from whose bourne no traveler returns, not because they cannot, but because they will not."

Despite his affection for his adopted territory, Kneeland's dreams and plans for Salubria never got off the ground. The town without a church and its godless philosophy did not appeal to the pioneer spirit. Iowans listened to Kneeland's views but did not join him. Few wanted to live in Salubria and it barely clung to life. The death blow came when Kneeland was elected chairman of the county Democratic convention and the voters of Van Buren County protested by soundly defeating the entire Democratic ticket in 1842.

For the next two years Abner Kneeland and his colony lost ground a little every day. By August of 1844 Kneeland, the man without a God, and Salubria, the town without a church, had both passed from this mortal world.

38

The Preacher and the Bell

Most folks around Iowa City in 1841 thought Michael Hummer was an odd soul, but they all admired his confidence and energy.

Hummer had organized the Presbyterian congregation in the frontier capital and was its first pastor. Accounts describe him as a serious, intellectual character who did not quite fit into frontier life. He also was said to have an "ungovernable temper."

It was this temper that got the preacher into trouble, upset the whole countryside, and causes his name to be remembered today.

When Hummer and his new congregation decided to build a church they were dismayed to find it would cost around $5,000. So the minister was sent East in hopes he could raise the money among older congregations. In return, Hummer was to receive expenses and ten per cent of the money collected.

After two years in the East, the energetic Hummer returned with enough money to build a church. And, best of all, he brought a bell with him.

For a frontier congregation a church with a bell was practically heaven on earth. The whole town was proud of the preacher and even prouder of the bell. It not only was the one church bell in Iowa City, it was said to be the first west of the Mississippi.

But Hummer had picked up something more than a bell during his journey. He had become interested in a weird religious doctrine called "Swedenborgianism," and soon became an enthusiastic convert. He also started dabbling in spiritualism and told friends he held regular communication with the departed.

These eccentricities did not set well with the people in Iowa City. After putting up with their peculiar preacher for some time, the congregation finally decided to oust him. In 1848 charges of misconduct were levied against Hummer.

A trial was held before the presbytery to consider the accusations. Things seemed to be going in Hummer's favor until he rose and dramatically announced that the congregation was a "den of ecclesiastical thieves." After this they practically kicked him out the door.

The unhappy Hummer departed for Keokuk where he said he planned to build a temple. Before leaving though, he obtained possession of the pulpit furniture, Bibles, and other movable property as part payment of the church's debt for unpaid salary. He also received a note for $650.

Once in Keokuk and dreaming of his new temple, Hummer remembered the bell. He had forgotten the bell! Here was a chance to get even with the ungrateful congregation and to obtain a bell for his new project.

Hummer and a friend left for Iowa City bent on revenge. They went to the church and the preacher crawled up a ladder into the belfry. The bell was then lowered with a block and tackle.

By this time word had spread through the town what Hummer was up to. While the preacher was in the belfry and his companion had gone to get a team and wagon, a crowd arrived and took down the ladder. The irate Hummer was imprisoned in the empty belfry.

While the preacher hurled pieces of boards and loose bricks, the jeering crowd made off with the bell. When Hummer's friend returned and rescued him the crowd and the bell were gone.

Thereafter began a long and farcical search for the missing bell. Hummer and his friend looked everywhere, muttering threats and curses as they searched.

Finally they consulted a lady with supposedly clairvoyant powers who told them the bell was in a well. But a damp investigation of every well in Iowa City failed to reveal the prized object. With heavy hearts, the two men left for Keokuk without revenge and without their bell.

Later Hummer sued the trustees for his unpaid salary and a settlement was made. The court then appointed a guardian for the preacher. The tribunal reasoned that since Hummer was in constant communication with the spirits of another world he was incompetent to care for matters in this world.

But what about the bell? After it had been taken from the church it was chained to an elm tree and sunk in Rapid Creek. However, when some of the abductors went to get it after the litigation was over, it was gone.

The story is that two Mormons who knew of the hiding place resurrected the bell and took it to Salt Lake City. As far as anyone knows it was never seen again in Iowa.

After all the excitement was over some Iowa City men wrote a song about "Hummer's Bell." Its last stanza goes:

> Ah, Hummer's Bell! Ah, Hummer's Bell!
> Hidden unwisely, but too well;
> Alas, thou'rt gone, thy silver tone
> No more responds to Hummer's Groan;
> But yet remains one source of hope,
> For Hummer left a fine bell rope,
> Which may be used, if such our luck,
> To noose our friend at Keokuk.

39

August Werner's Flying Machine

By anyone's standards, August Werner was a strange person. He had come to the little southwestern Iowa town of Imogene in the 1870's as an immigrant from Germany and still spoke with a thick accent. He was a quiet, withdrawn soul who spent much of his time alone, dreaming up ideas and gadgets. For August Werner was an inventor.

Actually, the immigrant was a skilled craftsman who made his living by working in his own woodworking shop. It is said that customers came for miles around because of his fine reputation.

But August's first love was really working on his own projects. Many times his customers would find they could not get work done because the little woodworker was too tied up completing some gadget of his own design. Naturally, people didn't like this and before long many started saying that August was a little "touched in the head."

As the days went by, August became even more seclusive and worked more and more in his backshop. Through the day and on into the night he would hammer and saw and glue, keeping the door locked from any outsiders. "What was August up to?" became the chief topic of conversation on the dusty streets of Imogene.

Then one day in 1886, August broke his silence and announced to the waiting world what he was doing. He was building an airplane!

To a world that was not to hear of the Wright Brothers for another seventeen years, this news surprised and mystified the townspeople. What in the world was an airplane?

For those curious enough to listen, Werner would take them to his dim, cluttered shop and display a small, carved model of what we would now call a helicopter. This, he would proudly proclaim, would soon cause man to fly in the air like a bird and take him hundreds of miles in a matter of hours.

August Werner's Flying Machine 131

Now those people in town who had doubted that August was crazy started to reconsider. Those who thought all along the inventor was "touched" started saying "I told you so."

But August went on with his work undaunted. Despite the scoffs and the snickers he toiled away hour after hour, and finally completed the machine that he was convinced would "fly like a bird."

He announced to one and all that on the Fourth of July holiday, 1886, he would make his flight and all interested were invited to attend. Needless to say the whole population of Imogene and much of the rural area were interested and most decided to go. This would be the laugh of the year.

Fate smiled on August by making the Fourth of July warm and clear. The usual excitement and activity of the holiday were secondary to the anticipation young and old held for the really big event of the day—August Werner's airplane ride.

That afternoon a group of men helped August carry his pride and joy to a steep cliff east of town. It was a weird-looking contraption, all fashioned from wood with a big propeller at top which was geared to pedals pumped by the pilot. It didn't look very sturdy.

By three o'clock a crowd of several hundred had gathered to watch the first flight of man. The great inventor surveyed the scene and decided to take advantage of the situation by making a little speech. He proclaimed to the onlookers that they were about to witness a history-making epoch. He planned to have dinner the next day in Washington with President Cleveland and supper the following day with the Kaiser in Berlin.

Then the big moment came. Werner crawled into the skeleton framework and started pedaling furiously. Gears creaked and cogs groaned as the big propeller slowly started to turn.

What actually happened next is a matter of dispute. One Charles Abbott, who died only a few years ago and was present at the time, said that the craft took off four feet above the ground. Others who were there swore it never left the earth.

But we do know the wooden cogs broke and Werner's machine didn't get far, if at all, off the ground. The thing actually fell to pieces before the very eyes of the people of Imogene. Hooting and laughing, the crowd went back to town. Alone and humiliated, August Werner sat among the ruins, a piece of broken propeller in his hands and a broken dream in his heart.

If August Werner had been of a different makeup he might have gone on and rebuilt his plane and been successful. But he wasn't. The jibes and the mockery, along with his failure, had been too much. A few months later his mind started to slip and he was taken to the mental institution at Clarinda. He remained there until death freed him, forty-five years later. While confined he continued his woodworking and was regarded as the finest craftsman around.

It's really too bad that Werner didn't succeed that day in 1886. For if he had his name would be known throughout the country instead of the Wright Brothers, and Imogene, Iowa, would be as famous as Kitty Hawk. Instead, Imogene dwells on in obscurity while poor August Werner is virtually forgotten.

But, while fame and fortune eluded August, he surely would be pleased today to see the tremendous strides in aircraft and to know that it is now possible to eat dinner in Washington and supper in Europe. And most of all, he would be happy to know the folks in Imogene have decided that maybe, just maybe, August Werner wasn't so crazy after all.

40

When Mrs. Bloomer Came to Iowa

Tongues were wagging one day in 1855 in Council Bluffs and kindly old ladies were outraged. Word had just been spread around town that a worldly and sinful influence was about to penetrate the straitlaced and upright village. If the devil himself had popped up right in main street the Council Bluffs citizens couldn't have been more surprised and indignant.

And what was this sinister and singular event? The object of Council Bluffs' ire was a pleasant, thirty-five-year-old matron whose name was known around the world for her "brazen and shameless" costume for women. Her name was Amelia Bloomer.

It had been just a few years before that Mrs. Bloomer had startled the nation when her temperance paper in Ohio, the *Lily*, started promoting a new dress for women. The costume consisted of a short dress that "reached scarcely to the knees" with "a full pantalet gathered in ruffles over the top of the shoe."

The mode of dress was sponsored by Mrs. Bloomer because she felt it was time for women to rebel against the domination of men in the matter of clothes. Dresses for the fair sex at that time were so uncomfortable, she claimed, that they sometimes deformed the wearer.

The new look swept America and was commonly called "bloomers." Men thought it brazen, women called it shocking and church groups condemned it. But women all over the country started wearing them and they even became popular in Europe.

Although most newspapers and magazines assailed Mrs. Bloomer's innovation, a few liberal publications upheld her. The editor of *Chamber's Edinburgh Journal* opined, "If the question is between the present skirts and Bloomerism, then we are Bloomerites." An admirer on the staff of *The Carpet-Bag* waxed poetically:

> The maids were very beautiful
> with ebon locks and tresses
> But what so much enhanced their charms
> were those short Bloomer dresses.

Mrs. Bloomer, serene and calm in the midst of the whirlwind of criticism, merely stated that a new day was dawning for American women and her dress was just a start on the many reforms that were to come.

She used her new fame to further the cause of abstinence and women's suffrage. Amelia traveled around the country, lecturing to groups and spreading the gospel of the right for women to vote. The Bloomer name was so well-known that requests poured in for her appearance.

Finally Amelia and her lawyer husband, Dexter, decided to strike out for the West in order to further his career.

Mr. and Mrs. Bloomer were surprised by the cool reception they received in Council Bluffs. But it didn't take long before they changed the attitude of the townspeople.

Actually, most people were a little taken aback when they met Mrs. Bloomer. Here was a woman whose name was known around the world because of a shocking new costume and she didn't seem at all like the flippant hussy most pictured her to be. Instead, Amelia Bloomer was a quiet, mild-mannered, courteous lady who exuded charm. In a short time she melted Council Bluffs' cold hostility with the warmth of her personality.

As the years passed the Bloomers not only were accepted in town but they became one of the most prominent families in western Iowa. Dexter's law practice flourished and he was known far and wide as a man of integrity. He was so highly regarded that the voters elected him mayor of Council Bluffs in 1869. Quite an achievement for a man who was shunned only fourteen years earlier!

Meanwhile, Mrs. Bloomer was busying herself carrying the banner for women's suffrage. In 1856 she addressed the Nebraska legislature so eloquently that they almost gave women the right to vote. "We expected to hear her rave and rant," commented the *Weekly Bugle* after one of her lectures, "but heard none of this. She was argumentative and even

The Bloomer Costume

eloquent in some of her remarks and had just enough sarcasm to them to spice them well." She later became president of the Iowa Women's Suffrage movement.

Amelia Bloomer was a gracious hostess and opened her home to many of the famous. The Hutchinson family, popular singers of the era, stopped by and suffrage leaders, Susan B. Anthony and Elizabeth Cady Stanton, enjoyed the hospitality of the Bloomer homestead.

Mrs. Bloomer never wore her famous costume after 1860. When asked why, she said it had served its purpose by focusing attention on the plight of women.

When Amelia Bloomer died on December 30, 1894, America lost a great champion of women's rights and Council Bluffs lost a true friend.

41

And Mary Rogan Got Dunked!

MARY ROGAN was a haughty soul. She was young, pretty and had a constant habit of speaking her mind regardless of the consequences. Her work at the Eureka House, a Mason City inn and stage stop in the 1860's, brought her in daily contact with many local residents who knew well her headstrong ways.

Mary was a controversial person in town. Although many admired her for her efficient and pleasant manner, many others disliked the young woman's loose tongue. But she didn't seem to mind and went about saying what she pleased when she pleased. It was the murder of Abraham Lincoln that really got Mary Rogan into trouble.

It was known all over town during the Civil War that Mary had southern sympathies. It was rumored she had relatives in the deep South and that she had been born there.

Although Mary would often make caustic comments about the North to anyone who would listen, most people paid little attention to her. Mason City residents tolerated the young lady and went about their business. Then word came in April, 1865, that Abraham Lincoln had been assassinated in Washington, D. C.

This news struck at the heart of Mason City. Lincoln was revered by the town. Four years earlier when the President had called for volunteers to join the fight to preserve the Union she was one of the first communities to respond. Only the very young or the very old and ill of the men were left in town during the war. During these heartbreaking years all looked to the tall, sorrowful man in Washington for leadership.

When word came by stage of Lincoln's death it stunned the frontier village as if one of their own had been lost. With bated breath and forlorn faces men and women gathered in little groups to discuss the

And Mary Rogan Got Dunked!

tragedy in Washington. Some felt the whole Civil War might have been fought in vain.

Many of these people gathered in the popular Eureka House to find out what little news arrived. It was here that Mary Rogan talked out of turn once too often.

She broke into a conversation about the martyred President with: "They say Lincoln has been shot. I hope to God it's true and I hope my brother shot him!"

Such treasonable talk astounded Mary's listeners. Before long her comments were being repeated in practically every home and store in town. This was going too far!

Women with husbands, brothers and sons in the Union Army seethed with indignation when they heard of Mary Rogan's comments. Here their menfolk had been fighting for their lives and a Confederate supporter lived right among them! By that evening the entire town was incensed by the words of the "terrible Rogan girl." Something had to be done.

"Let's duck her," someone suggested to a number of ladies gathered downtown. The idea caught on and was enthusiastically accepted. Quickly they formed together to start the march to Mary's home. The determined ladies added recruits along the way until they numbered over thirty.

One home they stopped at was the residence of Mrs. Elizabeth Kirk, one of the most prominent women of the town. Mrs. Kirk and her fourteen-year-old son answered the door and when told of the group's intentions they immediately offered their support. Mrs. Kirk had two sons in southern hospitals and one in a soldier's grave in Louisiana because of the war. She wasn't about to let a traitor live a peaceful life in Mason City! To add strength, the Kirk boy put on one of his mother's dresses and followed along.

Emotions were whipped into a frenzy by the time the women reached the Rogan home which stood on the corner of Fifth Street and Delaware Avenue North. They tramped up on the porch, burst through the door and led the surprised but unresisting Mary outside. Any attempt she might have made to run or fight was stifled when she saw the grim faces of her tormentors.

They hustled Mary down the main street walking in the street rather than on the narrow boardwalks that served as sidewalks. By now the victim was terrified and suddenly let loose with a piercing scream that could be heard for blocks around. Some unsuspecting men ran to see what was wrong but were told by the ladies that their presence was not needed. They stood gaping as the entourage passed by.

The women marched with their prisoner to shallow Willow Creek. While most of the group and much of the town watched from the bank, a few of the militant madams bodily forced Mary Rogan into the water.

A second and then a third time she was submerged while the growing crowd looked on. "My husband was fightin' rebels south and we will attend to them here," one soldier's wife shouted.

Up and down the struggling woman was dunked into the waters of Willow Creek. Finally the drenched Mary gasped and "begged pardon for what she had said and sacredly promised forever to be a good Union woman from that time forward, under all circumstance."

This satisfied the dunkers and they let her go up to the bank. Then they "blacked her face and would have sheared her head had she not earnestly entreated them not to do so, promising to be loyal." After this they administered to her the oath of allegiance, formed in procession and marched up Main Street singing. They stopped at McMillin's store where candies were passed to the crowd and a little celebration was held. W. E. Thompson, a former sailor and minister, was called upon for a speech and complied by congratulating the ladies for their loyalty. The crowd sang the Star Spangled Banner and then disbanded.

In all fairness to Mary Rogan it should be reported she kept her word about being loyal to the Union. Never again did she utter a sound that might rile up again the spirited women of Mason City.

42

Those Terrible Cherry Sisters!

Now that vaudeville has been dead for generations, most of the great acts and talented performers are forgotten. But almost everybody who ever saw a trio of girls called the Cherry Sisters will always remember them. For they were unanimously acclaimed by critics and audiences alike the worst act ever to hit the Great White Way.

There were five Cherry Sisters in all, but Effie, Addie and Jessie did most of the entertaining. They were all headstrong girls who grew up on a farm near Marion, Iowa. In order to attend the Chicago World's Fair in 1893, the sisters formed the Cherry Concert Company to raise money for the trip. They were given the free use of the Daniels' Opera House in Marion where they sang, delivered a comic ballad, read a tragic poem and imitated a Negro minstrel for two full hours. Everybody agreed it was an awful show but the girls ended up with $250 profit. They thought that wasn't bad for an evening's work and decided to make show business their career.

After sprucing up their act a little, the girls put on their second show a month later in an elegant showplace called Greene's Opera House in Cedar Rapids.

This program was notable in that much of the audience thought the sisters were so bad that they communicated this feeling in the way of apples, tomatoes, and eggs showered upon the stage. Although this conduct was far from dignified a newspaper defended the audience by saying:

Such unlimited gall as was exhibited last night at Greene's Opera House by the Cherry Sisters is past the understanding of ordinary mortals.

If some indefinable instinct of modesty could not have warned them that they were acting the part of monkeys, it does seem like the overshoes thrown at them would have conveyed the idea in a more substantial manner. . . .

Cigars, cigarets—everything was thrown at them, yet they stood there, awkwardly bowing their acknowledgments and singing on. Possibly the most ridiculous thing of the entire performance was an essay—think of it, an essay—read by one of the poor girls, in which she pled for the uplifting of the stage and hoped that no one would be harmed by anything they may have witnessed during the evening. The orchestra responded with 'Ra'ra'ra boom de ay.

But this unenthusiastic reception didn't daunt the Cherry Sisters. They packed their long dresses and took off for a tour of American cities. Wherever they went their show got front-page notices over all other news. One critic said they were "so bad they were good." People would line up hours before the sisters' show just to see if they were as bad as their reputation. Most agreed they were.

It was popular sport to throw vegetables at the girls. The *New York Times* even started referring to them as the "Vegetable Girls." A report was widely circulated that the Cherry Sisters often performed behind a screen of chicken wire to ward off items like ripe tomatoes and rotten eggs. But the girls always indignantly denied this. Addie once told a reporter, "We've never played behind a screen in our lives. I believe that we are the most misrepresented people in the United States. Reporters can't be trusted."

As the Cherry Sisters' fame grew so did their asking price. Because they always managed to draw a full house, theater managers clamored to sign the girls. Addie acted as business manager and it was said no man ever got the best of her on a financial deal. At times the sisters were drawing $1,000 a week. This was as much or more than many of vaudeville's finest performers were making and caused no little amount of resentment. The girls always claimed the jealousy of rivals was responsible for the vegetable treatment accorded them wherever they performed.

In 1901 the girls caused legal history by suing the *Des Moines Leader* for libel. The offending article made such comments as:

Effie is an old jade of fifty summers, Jessie a frisky filly of forty, and Addie, the flower of the family, a capering monstrosity of thirty-five. The mouths of their rancid features opened like caverns, and sounds like the wailings of damned souls issued therefrom.

In a decision that is quoted in legal textbooks all over the nation, the Court ruled against the Cherry Sisters after witnessing their act in the courtroom. Their theory, devoid of legal hodgepodge, was that the ladies were actually as bad as the newspaper had written!

When Jessie died in 1903, the Cherry Sisters retired and returned to Cedar Rapids to live. Later they opened a home bakery and did a thriving business for many years.

Effie, who was the domineering character, ran for mayor of Cedar Rapids in 1923 and 1925. Sister Addie was her campaign manager. Effie's platform was ". . . more paving, better water, a new city market, lower taxes and a curfew for all minors at 8:00 p.m." Despite a hard campaign, Effie was unsuccessful in her political ambitions.

From then on Effie spent much of her time writing. She authored three books: *The Old Blacksmith's Daughter*, *The Old Hermit's Daughter*, and *Ellanor*, all unpublished. She also wrote a play and said she planned to turn the play into a novel and her three novels into plays. The play also failed to ever reach print.

Although officially retired, Effie and Addie made personal appearances from time to time. As late as 1935 they appeared in a reenactment of their famous "mellerdrama," "The Gypsy's Warning," in New York City. Such famous showpeople as Tallulah Bankhead and Gracie Allen were among those who turned out to see what was left of the famous Cherry

Sisters. In these later performances the girls were always well received. Things had changed since their days in the theater.

None of the ladies ever married and it was always believed there had been no romance in their lives. Since they were very prim, righteous and demanding characters this was not surprising to those who knew them.

However, in 1943, one Carl Whyte who had been the piano player for the sisters told a newspaper that he had been in love with Effie even though she was twenty years his senior. Addie, he said, had come between them. He added, "I was completely hypnotized by her charms and her kisses took me completely out of this world." Whyte's claim was made after Effie's death and friends felt she would have vigorously denied such foolishness.

Whyte also said that the Cherry family included a brother who appeared with the girls once in 1896. But the booing and hooting, accompanied by the vegetable barrage, so upset the lad that he hopped aboard a freight loaded with hogs bound for Chicago and was never heard from thereafter.

Addie died in 1942 and the indomitable Effie passed away a few months later. The *New York Times* carried a full column article upon Effie's death and recounted for a new generation the story of the worst act in show business. After all, who could ever forget the Terrible Cherry Sisters?

PART SEVEN

Some Men We Can't Forget

43

Iowa's Frontier Governor

THE first governor of the Territory of Iowa looked like Andrew Jackson and by disposition and temper was a great deal like Old Hickory. Flowing gray hair combed up and back, high forehead, thin nose and blazing eyes were striking characteristics of Robert Lucas, appointed by President Van Buren in 1838 to serve as Iowa's leader. Not so evident traits included a code of morality higher than most preachers, a temper that could explode like a fire cracker and a stubborn streak as wide as the Mississippi.

By the time he wrapped up his Iowa career three years later, Lucas had incurred the wrath of the territorial assembly; made so many enemies they unsuccessfully petitioned the President for his removal; vetoed practically every measure dear to a legislator's heart; threatened our neighboring state of Missouri with war, and earned the respect of almost everybody as a good and able governor.

Robert Lucas was a Virginian by birth, an Ohioan by chance and an Iowan by choice. After moving to Ohio as a youth, Lucas was involved in many escapades and joined the Ohio militia to fulfill his zest for adventure. He served in the War of 1812 and later became a major general.

But politics got into Lucas' blood and he was elected to the Ohio legislature. As he gained prominence in the state Lucas was given many honors. In 1832 he was given the distinction of presiding over the first national convention ever held by the Democratic party. Later that same year he was elected governor of Ohio.

For four years Lucas served his state well. When he left office he had high hopes for appointment as United States senator, but was disappointed when he was bypassed in favor of a younger man. His dis-

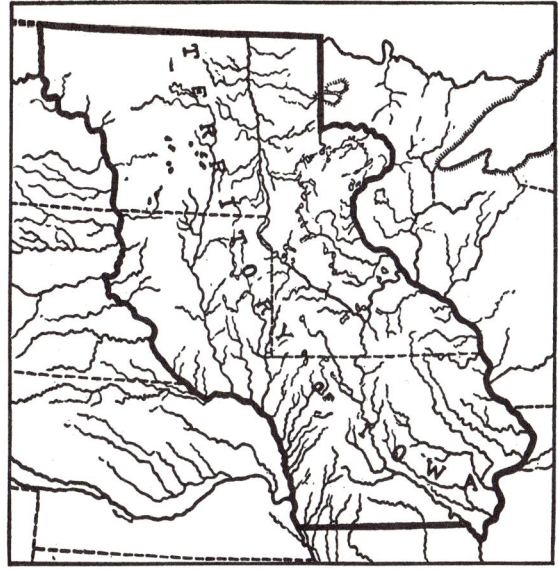

The Iowa Territory

appointment was short-lived however for he was soon offered the governorship of the Iowa Territory by President Van Buren. With enthusiasm and zeal renewed, Lucas started out for the long trip west.

When the new governor arrived, the Iowa Territory was much different from our present state. The area spread over a tract of land approximately three times the size of our state. The Canadian line was the northern boundary and the eastern half of North and South Dakota were included within its limits. Although the area was large the entire population was small—only around twenty-two thousand people, about one-tenth the size of present-day Des Moines. Burlington was the territorial capital and the General Assembly met in the Old Zion Church.

Lucas was fifty-seven years old when he reached Burlington and if he could have foreseen the events ahead of him he might have turned right around and gone back to Ohio.

His first conflict was with the secretary of the territory, William

Conway. Conway had arrived in Burlington before Lucas and had taken over many of the governor's duties. Conway, a young, ambitious man, was reluctant to drop any of his powers when Lucas arrived and relations between the two became very strained.

Besides his troubles with Conway, Lucas used his veto power several times in a running battle with the legislature. The governor was a thrifty man and scorned legislative extravagance.

He became particularly incensed over a bill that would provide a legislative staff of twenty-three janitors, clerks, firemen and sergeants-at-arms to serve the members. Lucas pointed out that there were only thirty-nine legislators and the staff would almost be as large as the body itself. He also vetoed a large salary bill for the lawmakers.

Besides vetoing their pet bills, Lucas criticized the representatives for their drinking, gambling and card-playing. Finally their resentment

Robert Lucas

became so great the legislature sent a petition to Washington asking for Lucas' removal, only to be refused by President Van Buren.

The most famous incident of Lucas' career was his role in the Iowa-Missouri border squabble known as the "Honey War." This time the governor had the solid backing of Iowans and the legislature, but angered the whole state of Missouri.

A dispute had developed between the two states over a thirteen-mile-wide tract of land along the border in what is now southern Iowa. Missouri claimed it and Iowa claimed it. Lucas told Missouri that their arguments should be taken to the United States Supreme Court and until settled otherwise the land would remain a part of the Iowa Territory.

Missouri did not heed the governor's words and, when she tried to collect taxes in the area by force, Lucas called out the state militia. Missouri did likewise and two hastily formed armies glared at each other for several hours near Farmington, Iowa, but no fighting developed. Finally both regiments went back home and the case eventually wound up in the hands of the Supreme Court which decided the land was rightfully Iowa's. The episode was called the "Honey War" because of the large number of bee trees loaded with honey in the area.

In 1841 the change of administrations in Washington caused Lucas' removal as governor and he retired from active politics. But he continued to serve his adopted territory by participating in the Constitutional Convention in 1844. He moved to the new capital, Iowa City, and lived there until his death in 1853 at the age of seventy-two. His fine brick home still stands in that city.

History has judged Robert Lucas as a firm, dedicated man who set a fine example of integrity and courage as Iowa's first governor.

44

Idol of the Roaring West

Of all the names of western heroes who are symbols of the wild and rugged West, none other is as famous as a white-haired Iowa native named William Frederick Cody. Cody's career was romanticized in story and song until he became a legend in his own time. His real name was forgotten but people on two sides of the ocean hailed him as "Buffalo Bill."

Billy Cody was born in 1846 near Le Claire, Iowa. He was a strong, active boy who liked to hold western shows in a neighbor's pasture, using an old black mare as his only animal.

When Billy was eight his father decided to seek his fortune farther west, packed all of his family's belongings in a covered wagon and set out for Kansas.

The Territory of Kansas was in turmoil over the slavery question when the Codys staked out their claim in Salt Creek Valley. Mr. Cody was against slavery and soon got into arguments with some of his neighbors. When Billy was ten he witnessed his father being stabbed in a fight by drunken, pro-slavery men.

From that time on young Cody learned to scout, as his family was constantly wary of attacks from his father's enemies.

In 1857, when Billy was eleven, his dad died as a result of the stab wound. The boy could now ride and shoot like a man so he got a job herding cattle to support his mother.

While helping drive cattle towards Fort Kearney, Billy and a group of men were attacked by Indians. They escaped by following the banks of a river but knew the red men were close behind. After dark, as the men were slowly making their way by the river, Billy saw the silhouette of an Indian ready to fire. The boy raised his rifle and fired, bringing

IDOL OF THE ROARING WEST   151

From the Painting by Rosa Bonheur

Buffalo Bill

the redskin down. At the age of eleven Bill Cody killed his first Indian and became a hero in the eyes of older men.

As Bill grew up he continued living on the plains. He worked on wagon trains and in 1860 became one of the first Pony Express riders in the country. He worked at this for two years, greatly improving his riding and shooting.

Cody enlisted in the Union Army in 1863 and served as a guide and scout. During a furlough he met Louisa Frederici in St. Louis and married her in 1866. For the first and last time in his life it looked like Bill Cody was going to settle down and live a peaceful existence. He and his bride returned to Leavenworth, Kansas, and ran a hotel. But this routine soon bored him and he went back to a life on the plains as a government scout.

After some unfortunate land speculation, Bill went to work for the Kansas Pacific Railroad as a buffalo hunter. He is reported to have killed 4,280 buffaloes within eighteen months and from that time on William Cody was known only as "Buffalo Bill."

Billy Comstock, a guide and scout, once claimed that he was king of the buffalo hunt and was rightfully Buffalo Bill. A contest was held between Cody and Comstock with the title and $500 at stake. Cody killed sixty-nine animals while Comstock bagged only forty-six. From that time on nobody ever challenged Buffalo Bill Cody.

Buffalo Bill, described as a "noble Vandyke stepped from its frame," gained fame because his friend, Ned Buntline, chose him as the hero for many of his Wild West stories. The writer urged Cody to go into show business and finally he agreed. He met Buntline in Chicago and in a matter of hours a play was written called "Scouts of the Plains." It was bad but the audience seemed to like the picturesque Westerner. One reviewer said he had heard the play was written in four hours and wondered why it had taken so long.

Buffalo Bill continued in western plays now and then until 1883 when he formed his own Wild West Show, complete with real Indians, guides, scouts, cowboys and bucking broncos.

The show opened in Omaha and became a tremendous success. Then it moved into Chicago and played to vast crowds. Buffalo Bill always received an ovation after every performance.

In 1896 the company leased Madison Square Garden and staged an even bigger production. Bill had many famous western characters appearing with him from time to time, including Sitting Bull, Wild Bill Hickok and Annie Oakley.

Then the extravaganza moved to London and took the town by storm. Twice Buffalo Bill played at the request of Queen Victoria.

Buffalo Bill's fame grew until his name was a household word. In 1898 a whole day was set aside to honor Cody at the Trans-Mississippi Exposition.

But by 1907 the great showman's health failed and his show went bankrupt. He went to work for the Sells-Floto Circus and later performed in the 101 Ranch Show.

His health worsened until death ended his remarkable career on January 10, 1917. He was buried on top of Lookout Mountain overlooking the great plains that had played such an important part in his life.

45

Jesse Raised an Apple Tree

Jesse Hiatt was a peaceful Quaker with a long stubborn streak who never gave up on anything he believed in. And a good thing, too, for if Jesse had been a quitter the world might never have known what many consider to be the finest apple ever grown—the Delicious apple.

Jesse lived on a half-section of land in Madison County in the mid-1850's. He and his wife, Rebecca, built a two-room log cabin and settled down to a life of farming and the raising of ten children.

The work was hard and the hours were long but within a few years the homesteaders began to prosper. Just after the Civil War Jesse was financially well off enough to build the largest barn in Madison County. Even when completed his bank account was by no means exhausted. Jesse and Rebecca decided to build a nice home to replace the log cabin.

However, Jesse's friends told him that he should use his money to build a flour mill and really make money. Wheat was supposed to be a good, stable crop at that time. So, Jesse took his savings, borrowed more at ten per cent interest and built the Centennial Mill.

For a couple of years the mill flourished but then troubles set in. The wheat crops failed, chinch bugs descended on the area and a long dry spell plagued the farmers. For over ten years Jesse Hiatt determinedly operated his mill at a consistent financial loss. During this depressing time in his life, Jesse turned to gardening to brightening his spirits. Events proved this was the wisest thing he ever did.

Folks around Winterset knew Jesse was quite a gardener. He already had produced two varieties of his own apples—the Hiatt Sweet and the Hiatt Black.

In the early 1870's Jesse noticed that a strange seedling was sprouting up between rows of another apple variety. Since it was out of line with the others Jesse cut it down. But it came up again. Jesse cut it down

JESSE RAISED AN APPLE TREE

again. Before long it appeared again and Jesse was so impressed with its hardiness that he left it alone.

For ten years Jesse nutured his wild seedling until it finally produced one lonely apple. The old farmer tasted it and smiled. "This is the best tastin' apple in the whole world," he proclaimed. For the rest of his life he was not to change his mind.

Jesse called his new apple the Hawkeye in honor of his home state. He worked and developed the seedling until it was producing a barrel of apples a year. Then he busied himself sending his Hawkeye apples to fairs and exhibits all over the Midwest. But usually the prizes went to the better known fruits. Wherever he went Jesse tried to persuade people that his apples were the best tasting in the world.

Eleven years after he had tasted that first apple things began to break for Jesse. He sent four specimens to the famous Stark Brothers Nursery Show in Louisiana, Missouri. C. M. Stark, one of the firm's founders, bit into the Hawkeye and immediately felt that here was a new and better apple.

But, as fate would have it, the name of the sender of the apples was lost and Stark had no idea who sent them or where they came from. His only course was to wait and hope the grower would try again the next year.

Jesse was disappointed in not hearing anything at all from the Stark show but he was not completely discouraged. After all, to a man who had spent twenty-one years working on one apple tree, another year didn't make much difference. The next year, 1894, he sent more Hawkeye apples to the Stark show and was immediately given a contract purchasing the propagation rights.

Stark renamed the Hawkeye the Delicious, a name he had long been carrying around in his head to give to the right fruit. Soon it became the most popular apple in the United States.

Jesse never said how much he got for the tree but it was more than enough to build the house he and Rebecca had wanted for so long. Jesse died before the dawn of the twentieth century but he lived to see his dream fulfilled. Today over ten million Delicious apple trees are in commercial orchards in the United States. Many, many more are in back yards and farm orchards

The original apple tree lived until 1940 when it was killed by a heavy frost. The next year new shoots sprouted from the old tree and they still grow near Winterset.

A large marker was erected in the Winterset City Park in 1922 honoring the Delicious apple and Jesse Hiatt—a fitting tribute to a stubborn tree that wouldn't die and a determined farmer who finally made the world agree that he had produced the "best tastin' apple in the world."

46

Ringling Brothers, Kings of the Circus

One day in 1870 a juggler and pole balancer from Dan Rice's Great Paris Pavillion Circus stopped in the harness shop in McGregor, Iowa. The leather belt with which he held a pole while an acrobat performed at the other end was broken and he wanted it repaired. Since the job was a minor one the shop owner fixed the broken strap and refused any payment. In appreciation the showman gave him a pass to the circus and invited the harness maker to bring his family.

The craftsman did attend the show with the four oldest of his seven boys. Although the father was not to realize it for many years to come, the destiny of his boys' lives was determined then and there.

The harness maker was August Ringling but his sons were to become known the world over simply as the Ringling Brothers, undisputed kings of the circus world.

The day after the big show, the young Ringlings rounded up yards of discarded rolls of wall paper, decorated them with figures of Bluebeards, Tom Thumb, Robinson Crusoe and other characters, mounted them on rollers and held a circus of their own.

A billy goat and neighborhood dogs were borrowed, a tent was erected of horse blankets and old carpets and, for the admission price of ten pins, youthful customers could see the very first Ringling Brothers Circus.

They say the Ringling boys' circus was quite successful, as childish performances go, and sawdust fever hit the youths hard. The brothers started working to achieve skills that could later be put to use in a show of their own.

Al, the oldest, is generally credited with starting the Ringling brothers on their way to fame. He became a juggler and tightrope walker and could perform the unusual feat of balancing a heavy plow on his chin.

In 1875, after the Ringling family had moved to Baraboo, Wisconsin,

Al had begun traveling with small shows. A few years later he was managing a little troop and in 1882 he decided to start out on his own. Calling upon brothers Alf and Charlie for help, the threesome formed the Ringling Brothers' Classic and Comic Concert Company. Later, John and Otto joined in the fun. For the rest of their careers these five men were associated with circus life.

The Ringling Brothers' first performance consisted of Al doing his tight-rope-walking act and topping this with his plow-balancing talent. Later, John would do an exhibition of balancing on a chair placed on glass bottles on a high stand. The other boys tooted horns to provide the music.

For two seasons the brothers trouped around Wisconsin and Iowa, building up their show and developing their skill as performers. Before long their show reached the stage where it required horse-drawn wagons for transportation. A trick horse and a bear were added and one great day the brothers added an elephant to their traveling menagerie.

As the circus grew, other performers were hired and the brothers handled the administrative details. It was a team effort all the way with each brother assigned a special job. The arrangement worked out well for over forty years without a scrap of paper ever existing as to any legal agreement.

John became the route agent and lined up the itinerary of the show. Alf took charge of publicity, Charles handled billings, Otto was the business manager and Al picked the acts and staged the performances.

The Ringling organization prospered. Other shows were bought out and merged into one and by the turn of the century the five Iowa brothers had one of the largest and most successful shows in the world.

In 1906 the Ringlings lived up to their own billing of gigantic, stupendous, overwhelming, colossal, spectacular, sensational, phenomenal and prodigious. For this year they purchased for nearly half a million dollars the famous Barnum and Bailey Circus and took the double name of Ringling Brothers—Barnum and Bailey.

An indication of the magnitude of the Ringling circus kingdom is shown by the fact that in its heyday the personnel of the show totaled over four thousand and it took two hundred forty full-length railroad cars to transport the show.

Ringling Brothers—Barnum and Bailey Circus played to millions of people and it is still regarded as the best show ever to perform under the big top.

Death invaded the ranks of the brothers and by 1930 only John Ringling was left. In the twilight of his career he stunned the show world by purchasing several other circuses and uniting them to make Ringling Brothers—Barnum and Bailey even bigger. He died in 1936.

Meanwhile, back in McGregor, every summer a new generation of small boys holds circuses of their own not far from the vacant lot where the Ringling brothers played many years ago.

47

"He Can Touch the Throne of God"

It had been a dull day the 1st of March, 1898, on the floor of the United States House of Representatives. Up for discussion was an appropriation bill providing aid for relatives of the sailors who lost their lives in the sinking of the Battleship Maine.

Then the Speaker of the House recognized Representative Robert Gorden Cousins from Iowa. The tall, powerfully built congressman started to speak.

No human speech can add anything to the silent gratitude, the speechless reverence, already given by a great and grateful Nation to its dead defenders and to their living kin.

Cousins' colleagues started to sit up and take notice at the poetic words and magnificent voice of this unknown representative from Iowa. Even the pages, who generally pay little attention to floor proceedings, stopped to listen.

Hovering above the dark waters of that mysterious harbor of Habana, the black-winged vulture watches for the dead, while over it and over all there is the eagle's piercing eye sternly watching for the truth.

By this time the House was quiet as a tomb as everyone present listened in awe to the thrilling speech. Building to a crescendo, Cousins concluded with:

> *The tumult and the shouting die*
> > *The Captains and the Kings depart*
> *Still stands thine ancient sacrifice,*
> > *An humble and a contrite heart.*
> *Lord God of Hosts, be with us yet,*
> > *Lest we forget—Lest we forget.*

"He Can Touch the Throne of God"

The next day newspapers and colleagues were singing the praises of the Iowa orator. Senator Dolliver said: "Why, he can reach up, with perfect ease, and touch the very throne of God."

The *Louisville Courier-Journal* called Cousins ". . . a mystery. He seldom speaks, but is the finest orator in Congress." The *Philadelphia Star* commented: "When Mr. Cousins sat down amid the storm of cheers, which again and again swept the room, Senator Edmunds advanced and congratulated him on having made the best speech he had ever heard." And the *Chicago Tribune* said Cousins' oration ". . . will be preserved as one of the gems of American oratory."

Back in Cousins' hometown of Tipton, in Cedar County, folks really weren't too surprised to hear of their local boy's sudden fame. Those who had known young Bob Cousins always thought he was destined for great things.

As a boy Cousins had been a student of history and a lover of music and art. At seventeen he had gone to Cornell College at Mount Vernon and graduated in 1881 with an engineering degree. Later he became interested in law and worked in a Cedar Rapids attorney's office to study for the bar. After practicing a few years in Audubon, Iowa, and South Dakota, Cousins returned to Tipton.

The home folks demonstrated their high regard for the young lawyer by electing him to the Iowa House of Representatives in 1885, on the Republican ticket. At twenty-six, he was the youngest member of the General Assembly.

In 1892 Cousins was sent to Congress and served with distinction for sixteen years. His reputation as an orator steadily grew during this tenure and he became one of Washington's most popular congressmen.

He always was very much in demand in the social whirl of Washington. "If he had set the hearts of Tipton belles aflutter when ocasionally he had whisked them away on Sunday evenings for a buggy ride, his presence at a ball made the Washington belles quite as twittery," a newspaper commented.

There was a rumor at one time that Congressman Cousins was engaged to the daughter of Speaker of the House Thomas Reed. However, the wedding never materialized and Cousins remained a bachelor all his life.

Although the Iowan was a genial man, his ire could be aroused. Once the Iowa Republican party platform took issue with the protective tariff, which Cousins strongly believed in.

A report was circulated that the congressman had called his own party's declaration a "dirty, lousy lie." A group of concerned party leaders met with Cousins and asked him to make a statement.

He slowly looked around the room, paused and then said: "Gentlemen, I didn't say what I am reported to have said, but what I am reported to have said is the truth. That platform IS a dirty, lousy lie—and I'm going to stand or fall on what they say I said."

That fall, Cousins was reelected by one of the largest majorities he ever received.

The Iowa congressman surprised everybody in 1908 when he announced his retirement from politics. He was only forty-nine years old.

Cousins returned to Tipton and lived in his quiet, bachelor quarters. He came out of his self-imposed seclusion only occasionally to give a lecture or speak in eulogy of a departed friend. For the most part he lived alone among his books and memories.

Among his items of the past were invitations to receptions by Theodore Roosevelt and Grover Cleveland.

On a cold January morning in 1931, friends found the now white-haired orator unconscious in his room. He was taken to the University Hospital at Iowa City where he remained until his death two years later at the age of seventy-four. Burial took place in a little country cemetery in Cedar County, five miles south of Stanwood.

At Cousins' funeral a strange tribute was read that had been written years earlier by Charles Wheeler, a Cedar Rapids attorney and a close friend of Cousins. When both Wheeler and Cousins had been in failing health they agreed to write each other a tribute to be read at their respective funerals. Mr. Cousins read his at Wheeler's services in Cedar Rapids in 1927.

The Wheeler oration, read by Henry Adams, a Des Moines lawyer, said:

I knew the man whose body lies here for many years and walked with him. He was much. He might have been everything. A great

"HE CAN TOUCH THE THRONE OF GOD"

brain, a tongue of gold, a Hercules physically, but the poison that lies in the heart of the corn invaded his body and caused him to fall before his time.

It robbed his friends of his love and companionship. It robbed the world of his thoughts. It robbed the English-speaking people of an orator. It robbed literature of his writings. It robbed the dumb animals of a lover. It robbed humanity of a man who could look at the stars, the flowers and the sunshine and smile and understand.

And so in his behalf I give, devise and bequeath his love of music to the song birds, his eloquence to all who speak the English tongue, his body to the flowers, his soul to immortality, and his memory to those who loved him. Peace, eternal peace to his ashes.

48

Into the Wild Blue Yonder!

When Mrs. Franklin Robinson came to Grinnell in 1896 with her four children, people noticed that twelve-year-old Billy was a mechanical whiz.

He could mend broken items around the house, repair all the ancient bicycles in the neighborhood and he loved to build various contraptions in the tool shed.

Everybody thought the boy would apply his technical ability in his later years and perhaps really go places. But in 1896, nobody could have dreamed just how far Billy Robinson would go.

Billy was a small boy and even at maturity was not a large man. He was quiet and courteous but he had an intense fire and drive that caused him to apply himself relentlessly to any project he undertook. Whenever talk came around to mechanical things, Billy's eyes would light up and his enthusiasm would bubble over.

As Billy grew up in Grinnell he was apprenticed to the local handyman and soon became as proficient as his employer. When his family moved away, Billy stayed on in town and worked at the shop for his keep.

Around 1905 Billy and a friend bought the repair shop. Now that he was the owner, the youthful inventor could experiment with his own ideas.

The main interest of Billy Robinson centered around his dream of constructing a flying machine. Working alone and by his own design, he molded castings, welded iron and built a frame for his first machine.

His engine was a failure and went to pieces but he kept trying and produced a motor that eventually became the pattern for later engines.

In 1910, as Billy put the finishing touches on his masterpiece, a traveling show came to town. He decided this was a good time to demonstrate his craft and arranged to take it to the fairgrounds. The flimsy monoplane, boasting a sixty-horsepower radial engine and shiny new paint,

Billy Robinson

was the hit of the show. Billy didn't attempt to launch the plane but nobody seemed to mind.

When the show left town the next day, Billy and his plane went with it, by request of the manager.

The young inventor realized that a plane wasn't much good without a pilot so he decided to take up the new skill of flying. Max Lily, a well-known aviator, gave Billy a year of lessons in Florida.

When he mastered this, Billy went to Chicago and worked as an instructor in an aviation school. In 1911 he became a partner in the National Aeroplane School, where he remained until 1913 when he returned to Grinnell.

Back home the twenty-nine-year-old flyer became one of central Iowa's best known men around 1914-15. His sputtering plane was a familiar sound to residents in a fifty-mile radius of Grinnell. Whenever they heard that unmistakable roar of the engine, men, women and children rushed to their doors and windows to see Billy sailing in the sky. "That Bird Man's at it again!" they would shout.

And Billy was a figure of admiration around town, too. After all, with his own brains and ingenuity he had conquered the air. Not many men in the whole United States could say that!

So many people had confidence in Billy that when he organized the Grinnell Aeroplane Company they rushed to buy stock. If just a little bit of luck had been riding on the wing with Billy Robinson, Grinnell might have become an aviation center. But this was not to be.

For a while things went well for the young aviator. On October 1, 1914, he established a nonstop flight record from Grinnell to Kentland, Indiana, a distance of some three hundred ninety miles in four hours forty-four minutes. The previous nonstop record at that time was one hundred twenty-five miles.

Billy also became the second authorized carrier of air mail by delivering a bag of letters from Des Moines to Grinnell. When he sailed over his hometown, whistles tooted and crowds roared as the whole town cheered him on.

But Billy Robinson's luck ran out on the bright blue day of March 11, 1916. He was trying to establish a new altitude record, which was then seventeen thousand feet. While his wife and many others looked on, Billy set out in a southeasterly direction, steadily going higher and higher.

Then the residents watching near the little town of Ewart heard a miss in the distant roar of the engine. Billy's biplane could be seen pathetically twisting and turning like a leaf falling from a tree. Down and down the little craft plummeted, followed by a splintering crash. No longer would Billy Robinson roam the Iowa skies.

In Hazelwood Cemetery at Grinnell there stands a granite slab bearing a bronze tablet that pays tribute to Iowa's pioneer aviator. It reads:

This stone marks the resting place

of

WM. C. ROBINSON

Pioneer nonstop flier and second
authorized carrier of air mail.
He met his death in his plane a few
miles south of Grinnell when making
an altitude flight March 11, 1916.
Erected by those who honor the
memory of Billy Robinson.

49

When Bryan Came to Iowa

Around the turn of the century, the biggest day in the lives of thousands of rural Iowans was the day the Chautauqua came to town.

The Chautauqua was a varied program of speeches and music with performers who traveled from village to village. Its name was derived from Chautauqua Lake, New York, where the first program was held.

It was always a day of joy when the Chautauqua arrived. People came to the show, usually held at the fairgrounds, on horseback and by various types of horse-drawn vehicles. A few dusty horseless carriages could even be found. The scene was gay with bright colors and flags flying. Many brought their lunches in boxes under their arms or cooked over open campfires. Some camped on the grounds for the full length the Chautauqua stayed in town. The whole thing took on the aspect of a holiday.

The programs were given for a week with different entertainers every day and a show each afternoon and evening. Some of the bills might feature musicians like Paderewski, Ernestine Schumann-Heink, The Golden Jubilee Singers or the popular Weatherwax Brothers of Charles City, Iowa.

For the main feature a lecture would be presented by a humorist or politician. James Whitcomb Riley, Strickland Gillan and Opie Read gave amusing talks around the state, while men like Champ Clark or William Howard Taft contributed to the political side of the Chautauqua.

For a world without radio or television, the Chautauqua was educational, colorful and entertaining.

One of the most celebrated of all Chautauqua lecturers was William Jennings Bryan of Lincoln, Nebraska. Bryan was a robust, handsome man with a beautiful stentorian voice that could be heard on the outer reaches of any crowd in those days before loudspeakers.

William Jennings Bryan Speaking at Allerton, Iowa, in the Early 1900's

Bryan had won the Democratic Presidential nomination in 1896 on the strength of one speech, his famous "Cross of Gold" oration. Before then he was just an unknown, thirty-six-year-old congressman from Nebraska. After his thrilling speech his name was known around the world. From that time on, until his death in 1925, Bryan was to remain in the public eye. Although defeated three times for the presidency, the "silver-tongued orator" held a large block of followers that worshipped his every deed.

Across the windswept Iowa prairies "The Great Commoner," as his brethren called Byran, made appearances in such places as Storm Lake, Fairfield, Indianola, Columbus Junction, Allerton—and dozens of other Iowa communities. Rock-ribbed Hawkeye Republicans wouldn't vote for Bryan, but whenever he made an appearance they flocked to hear him.

Through the scalding Iowa heat, Bryan would deliver his lectures with all the dramatics and vocal tricks that God had given him. Even though his speeches were often two hours long his audience would forget the heat and the dust while they hung on every word.

When Bryan Came to Iowa

Can you imagine Bryan, with his arm forward in a sweeping gesture and his magnificent voice roaring to the heavens, as he spoke these words from his famous religious lecture, "The Prince of Peace"?

If the Father deigns to touch with divine power the cold and pulseless heart of the buried acorn and to make it burst forth from its prison walls, will he leave neglected in the earth the Soul of Man, made in the image of his Creator?

No, I am sure that he who ... created nothing without a purpose, and wasted not a single atom in all His creation, has made provision for a future life in which man's universal longing for immortality will find its realization. I am as sure that we live again as I am sure that we live today.

An Iowan with fond memories of Bryan is Grant Perrin of Marion, Iowa. Mr. Perrin wrote of meeting Bryan at a Chautauqua in 1908, near Charles City. Perrin was ten years old at the time. After the introduction, "The Great Commoner" asked the boy, who was nearly blind, if he had any sight at all. When Perrin answered, "A little," Bryan pulled out a silver dollar and said, "I am going to throw something on the ground. See if you can find it."

Perrin got down on the ground and soon came up with the money. When he handed it back, Bryan refused it saying, "Keep it, and show it to your friends. Always remember it is a piece of Bryan silver."

Today, Mr. Perrin still has the silver dollar.

The Chautauqua circuit flourished for many years in the Midwest, but started to decline in the 1920's. When people started buying crystal sets to listen to KDKA in Pittsburgh and other stations that started sprouting up, the Chautauqua died a certain death.

But there are thousands of Iowans today who cherish memories of the days when they would do the chores early, pack a lunch of fried chicken and homemade bread, and go to town to spend the day at the Chautauqua. Most of all, for those who heard William Jennings Bryan, they remember the golden voice of "The Great Commoner" still ringing through the years.

50

Billy Sunday, Voice of the Sawdust Trail

In those quiet years at the turn of the century, the most energetic foe of sin and the devil was an Iowa orphan who grew up to be the greatest evangelist of them all.

Billy Sunday was his name and never before or never since has America seen the likes of a preacher with more fire and brimstone. He raised millions of dollars for charity, caused over a half-million sinners to answer his call to faith, blistered the hides of his critics and dried up liquor traffic in twelve states. He added the phrase "hit the sawdust trail" to our language and his colorful antics packed tabernacles from Maine to California.

And it all started because Billy Sunday liked to play baseball.

Billy was born in 1862 in a log cabin near Ames. A month after his birth Billy's father was killed in the Civil War and his widow was left the task of raising her three boys alone. Theirs was an impoverished existence and when Billy was twelve he was sent to an orphan's home at Glenwood and then to Davenport.

When the boy left the Davenport orphanage he boarded with Senator John Scott of Nevada. During his years in Nevada High School and after his graduation in 1881, Billy gained local fame for his baseball prowess.

A scout for the Chicago White Sox saw him playing at Marshalltown and signed Billy. The Iowa boy went into the big time and did all right for seven years. He is credited with being the first man to run the sacks in fourteen seconds. His speed was so great that he stole two hundred fifty-eight bases during his career; ninety-six bases in one season.

According to Billy, he spent some time during his baseball days in saloons and liked a glass of beer now and then.

One evening after making the rounds of a few Chicago saloons, Billy

Billy Sunday

and several ballplayers sat down on a curb to rest. A mission band was playing nearby and they struck up a tune that had been a favorite of Billy's mother. This so stirred him that he decided to join the church and became an active worker. In 1891 he gave up a $500 a month baseball contract to work at the Chicago Y. M. C. A. at $83.33 a month.

The next few years Billy worked as an advance man for a traveling evangelist. Then the evangelist quit and young Sunday was thrown out of a job with no way to support his wife and family.

But, as he said later, "I laid it before the Lord and in a short while there came a telegram from Garner, Iowa, asking me to come out and conduct some meetings. I didn't know anybody out there and I don't know yet why they ever asked me to hold a meeting, but I went."

His debut there in 1896 started Billy Sunday on a career that was to make him the most famous preacher of his time. Seven years later he was ordained a Presbyterian minister.

When Billy gave a sermon he didn't just talk. He would jump, leap, wrestle, shed his coat and tie, and pound folding chairs to kindling.

"When I'm through (fighting liquor) men will be so dry they'll have to be primed before they can spit," he shouted.

His listeners loved him and showed their affection by generously contributing to the washtub that was passed around for donations.

The theme of most Sunday sermons concerned the devil, liquor and the decline of the modern generation. Billy carried a red kitchen chair on his travels and wrestled with it to illustrate man's struggles with sin.

On the last night of his stay in a town Billy would preach against delaying the call to God. He would entreat:

Tonight, when the last song is sung, the last prayer said and we have all passed out into the night and Fred has switched off the lights—your chance, sinner, will be gone. My God, if the Lord would only draw back the veil which is between you and your coffin, you would leap back in horror to find it so near that you could reach out and touch it. But you say, tomorrow.

As Billy zoomed to fame and popularity in the early 1900's, some more conventional ministers criticized his circus-like approach to religion.

But Billy sneered at his critics and shot back that the church needed fighting men, not ". . . hog-jowled, weasel-eyed, sponge-columned, mushy-fisted, jelly-spined, pussy-footing, four-flushing, charlotte-russe Christians."

Billy's popularity waned somewhat after the first World War but he continued evangelistic work until the early 1930's. He died in Chicago in 1935.

Billy Sunday's ties to his home state of Iowa were strong throughout his life. His initials are carved in the bell tower at Nevada's old school and his widow visited Nevada during its centennial celebration in 1953.

He liked to say:

I was bred and born in old Iowa. I am a rube of the rubes. I am a hayseed of the hayseeds. The malodors of the barnyard are on me yet it beats Pinaud and Colgate, too. I have drunk coffee out of a saucer and eaten with my knife.

I expect to get to heaven, just the same.

And no one doubted that Billy Sunday was right again.

Index

A
Adams, H. P., 29-30
"American Gothic," 120-122
Artesian Well, 74-76
Audubon County, 37
Aviation, 130-132, 164-166

B
Bad Axe River, 10
Barnum & Bailey Circus, 158
Barnum, P. T., 82
Belle Plaine, 74-76
Bellevue, 34-36
Black Hawk, 8-10
Black Hawk War, 8-10
Bloomer, Amelia, 133-135
Boone County, 23-25, 98
Bradford, 66
Britt, 68-70
Brown, John, 92-94
Brown, William, 34-36
Bryan, William J., 167-169
"Buffalo Bill" Cody, 150-153
Bulwer, F., 106-107
Burdette, Bob, 112-113
Burlington, 10, 147

C
"Calico Road," 29-30
Cardiff Giant, 80-82
Carpenter, C. C., 89-90
Cass County, 110
Cedar County, 92, 161
Chautauqua, 167-169
Cherry Sisters, 140-143
Cody, William, 150-153
Coomes, Oll, 110-111
Coppoc Brothers, 92-94
Corn Palace, 77-79
Cousins, Robert, 160-163
Cowles, Gardner, 82
Coxey's Army, 117

D
Davenport, Colonel George, 36
Davenport Gazette, 30-31
Decatur County, 40, 42, 46-49

Delaware County, 104
Delicious Apple, 154-156
Dewey, Admiral, 70
Dillinger, John, 57-59
Duncombe, John, 22, 89, 91

E
Eclipse of Sun, 71-73
Eldon, 120-122

F
Fayette County, 14
"Female Flying Pigeon," 11-13
Foreman, John, 43-45
Fort Des Moines, 29
Fort Dodge, 21-22
Fort Madison, 4-7

G
Gardner, Abigail, 26-28, 89
Gardner Family, 26-28
Gear, Governor, 42
Greene County, 43
Grimes, Governor, 88, 95-97

H
Hamilton County, 22
Hamilton, Lt. Thomas, 5, 6
Hancock County, 68
Harlan, Senator James, 96
Harpers Ferry, Va., 92-94
Hiatt, Jesse, 154-156
Homer, 20-22, 25
Honey Creek, 98
"Honey War," 148-149
Hull, George, 80-82
Humboldt County, 24
Hummer, Michael, 127-129

I
Impeachment Trial, 95-97
Indian Wars, 8-10
Inkpaduta, 25, 26-28, 88
Iowaville, 10, 11
Iowa City, 31
Iowa Territory, 146-149
Iowa Tribe, 11-13

J

Jackson County, 34
Johnson, President, 95-97
Jones County, 43-45

K

"Kelly's Army," 117-119
Keokuk, Chief, 9
Kirkwood, Governor, 94
Kneeland, Abner, 124-126

L

Lake Okoboji, 25
"Le Claire, Antoine," The, 30
Lincoln, Abraham, 102, 136
Little Brown Church, 65-67
Little Cedar River, 66
"Little Hill," 14
Logan, Frederick Knight, 114-116
London, Jack, 117-119
Lott, Henry, 23-25
Lott, Milton, 23-25
Louisa County, 19
Lucas, Governor Robert, 146-149
Lyons-Iowa Central Railroad, 29-30

M

Mahaska, Chief, 11-13
Mason City, 57-59, 136-139
Massey, Louisa, 18-19
Massey, Woodbury, 17-18
McCreery, John L., 104-107
Mercer Brothers, 40-42
"Missouri Waltz," 115-116
Moingona, 98-99

N

Nashua, 66, 67
Newcastle, 21, 22
Nutting, Reverend John, 67

O

Old Zion Church, 147
Omaha Indians, 12
Otoe Indians, 13

P

Pashepaho, Chief, 9
Pea's Point, 24
Pitts, William S., 65-67

R

Railroads, 29-31
Rantchewaime, 11-13
Ringling Brothers, 157-159
"Roaring Cloud," 28
Robinson, Billy, 164-166
Rock River, 8
Rogan, Mary, 136-139

S

Sac and Fox Indians, 8
Salubria, 125-126
Saukenuk, 8
Scarlet Point, 26-28
Sharp, Abigail Gardner, 26-28
Shelby County, 38
Shelley, Kate, 98-99
Siam, 54-56
Sidominadota, 23-25
Sioux City, 77-79
"Sleep, Old Pioneer," Frontispiece
Spirit Lake, 62-64, 88-91
Spirit Lake Massacre, 25, 26-28, 88
Sullivan Brothers, 100-102
Sunday, Billy, 170-172

T

Taylor County, 54-56
Tegarden Massacre, 14-16
Territorial Capital, 147
"There Is No Death," 104-107, 108-109
Troublesome Creek, 37
Troublesome Gang, 37-38

U

"Under Hawkeye Skies," 2
U.S.S. Iowa, 83-85
U.S.S. Juneau, 100-102

V

Van Buren County, 125-126
Villisca Axe Murders, 50-53

W

Webster County, 20-22, 25
Werner, August, 130-132
"White Cloud," 11-13
Williams, Major William, 88-91
Winnebago Indians, 14-16

Wisconsin Territory, 19
Wood, Grant, 120-122

Y

Yellow Medicine River, 28